THE FALL OF THE SHAH

FEREYDOUN HOVEYDA

Translated by Roger Liddell

WYNDHAM BOOKS

NEW YORK

Copyright © 1979 by Fereydoun Hoveyda
Translation © 1980 by George Weidenfeld & Nicolson Limited
All rights reserved
including the right of reproduction
in whole or in part in any form
Published by *Wyndham Books*
A Simon & Schuster Division of
Gulf & Western Corporation
Simon & Schuster Building
1230 Avenue of the Americas
New York, New York 10020
WYNDHAM and colophon are trademarks
of Simon & Schuster
Designed by Stanley S. Drate
Manufactured in the United States of America

10 9 8 7 6 5 4 3 2 1

Library of Congress Cataloging in Publication Data

Hoveyda, Fereydoun.
The fall of the Shah.

1.   Iran—Politics and government—1941–1979.
2.   Hoveyda, Fereydoun.   3.   Diplomats—Iran—
Biography.   I.   Title.
DS318.H6713   955'.053   80-199

ISBN 0-671-61003-1

CONTENTS

He ended fearing for his life, on the pinnacle
of nothingness.

—OWHADI (twelfth century)

This is the excellent foppery of the world,
that, when we are sick in fortune, often the
surfeits of our own behaviour, we make guilty
of our disasters the sun, the moon, and
stars . . .

—SHAKESPEARE, *King Lear,*
Act I Scene 2

PROLOGUE

Orly, France, Tuesday, October 3, 1978

Beneath an overcast sky, the huge metal carcass gently settles on the landing strip. The Boeing slows and turns toward its parking point. Finally it rolls to a halt, and the hatch slowly opens.

Framed in the doorway a bizarre-looking man now appears, like a traveler from the fourth dimension lost in a century different from his own. Airport officials and air hostesses turn curious eyes upon him. What distant time produced this black-turbaned figure with the long white fake-looking beard? His eyes hard and unblinking under bushy eyebrows, he takes a few short steps toward his waiting friends, who at once surround him and lead him into the maze of airport buildings. The police officer examines his passport and reads the name of Rouhollah Moussavi Khomeini.

The group passes through customs, walks downstairs and makes for the exit, stopping for a moment on the concourse, near the marble slab engraved with

General de Gaulle's words describing the airport as a place for "the meeting of earth and sky."

The Ayatollah is joining the men of the opposition. Religion is taking its place at the heart of the revolution. Earth and sky are meeting!

Tehran, Iran, Tuesday, October 3, 1978

The summits of the Elburz glow in the setting sun. In his palace at the foot of the imposing mountain range, Mohammad Reza Pahlavi, Light of the Aryans, Shahanshah of Iran, rubs his hands in delight at having at last got rid of the man who has been a thorn in his side ever since being exiled to Najaf, across the border in Iraq. At a distance of four thousand miles he will no longer be able to spread subversion in the country. The King of Kings smiles with relief: once again he has managed to outfox his opponents. He sends a congratulatory telegram to his Foreign Minister, in New York attending the General Assembly of the United Nations, because it was he who negotiated the expulsion of the Ayatollah with his Iraqi colleague, on the sovereign's instructions.

The Shahanshah, Light of the Aryans, successor to Reza Shah, second in the line of the Pahlavi dynasty, does not yet suspect that this third of October marks the beginning of the end not only of his own reign but of twenty-five centuries of monarchy in Iran.

The move to Neauphle-le-Château, a few miles from the center of Paris, suddenly thrusts Khomeini into the foreground of international politics. Thanks to TV, radio and the press he becomes a world figure, and his messages reach the Iranian masses even more easily than before. The organized opposition long based in Europe in order to elude the repression of SAVAK (the Shah's secret police) flocks around the Ayatollah, rallies to him and works out a program of government. In Najaf the Ayatollah had not enjoyed the same freedom as in France. The Iraqi authorities had kept him under close surveillance, restricted the number of his visitors, and not allowed foreign correspondents to get near him.

From October 3 onward the tempo of events quickens. The duel between the Shah and Khomeini takes on a new dimension. It is as if the two protagonists in the drama were resuming a game of chess interrupted fifteen years before. Now it is Khomeini's move. The Shah sits waiting, brimful of confidence in the future.

The hostility between the two men goes a long way back. Iran's Shi'ite community always despised the first of the Pahlavis, Reza Shah, but came to terms with him because it could not openly oppose him. Restored to his throne in 1953 by the *coup d'état* staged by General Fazlollah Zahedi with CIA support, inside ten years Mohammad Reza Shah had rid himself of the chief ministers imposed on him by the Americans. Having finally taken absolute power, in the early 1960s he launched his program of agrarian reform and modernization. The reaction was not slow to materialize, and the most violent opposition came from Khomeini, who called on the faithful to rebel. Rioting broke out in Tehran in 1963, and was bloodily repressed by the Shah, who threw Khomeini into jail. The religious community agitated and protested, and to calm them the sovereign exiled the Ayatollah, who settled in Najaf after a brief stay in Turkey. So the Shah had won the first round. But Khomeini was just as obdurate a character as his enemy, and he did not consider himself beaten. As he left Iran he murmured, "We shall see whose word the people will follow, mine or the Shah's." Is there not a verse of the Koran which proclaims that Allah is on the side of the patient? Fifteen years later the struggle between the two men resumed in earnest.

It is a curious fact that both the Shah's success in 1963 and the Ayatollah's in 1979 were confirmed by referenda with majorities of ninety-five percent: the first in favor of the monarchy and of modernization, the second in favor of the Islamic Republic and against modernization. Whether this was a case of emulation or of pure coincidence is unimportant. What is interesting is the total reversal, in the space of fifteen years, of the aspirations of an entire people. How and why did that reversal take place? That is what I am going to try to elucidate, as objectively as I can, by retracing the events of the final months of imperial rule and by drawing on my own recollections. I hope that the reader of these pages will forgive me in advance if I am sometimes overcome with emotion. I cannot forget the murder of my brother, former Prime Minister Amir Abbas Hoveyda, subjected as he was to a parody of justice, despite the assurances given by the Ayatollah to the President of France.*

_____

* President Giscard d'Estaing referred to this promise at a press conference in April 1979.

1

THE BEGINNING
OF THE END

Nobody can overthrow me. I have the
support of 700,000 troops, all the workers
and most of the people.

—Mohammad Reza Pahlavi,
U.S. News and World Report,
June 26, 1978

Tehran, Iran, Sunday, December 31, 1977

President and Mrs. Carter, en route to India, saw the New Year in with the Shah at the Niavaran Palace. This visit intrigued the journalists. The two men had actually met a month previously in Washington. So what did this stop-off mean? The truth was that the President of the United States, whose Administration had sometimes criticized the dictatorial regime in Iran, wanted to make a public show of support. He was bringing the Shah a statement of his satisfaction over the question of human rights. At midnight the two heads of state exchanged toasts with a clink of crystal glasses. Champagne flowed freely. Carter celebrated Iran's rapid progress and expressed his admiration to the enlightened monarch who enjoyed "his people's total confidence."

Less than a year later, hundreds of thousands of Iranians took to the streets in practically every major town, to shouts of "Death to the Shah!"

How could a man as well informed as the President of the United States be so utterly wrong? Yet the bomb placed by the door of the American Cultural Center in Tehran the previous day constituted a clear warning, and as recently as December 29 the information agencies had announced the closing to the public of the motorway leading from Mehrabad Airfield to the imperial palace, and the occupation by the police of all the houses and apartments along the way. Moreover, masked demonstrators had already shouted, "Death to the Shah!" just a few steps from the White House lawn in November. Of course, another group had given the sovereigns a lukewarm welcome not far away, but everybody knew that Ambassador Ardeshir Zahedi (the General's son and the Shah's former son-in-law) and SAVAK agents had been scouring the Iranian embassies and consulates to recruit "volunteers." Furthermore, the President could not fail to be aware of the criticism of the Shah's regime voiced loud and clear in America's universities and mass media. Professors like Richard Cottam of the University of Pittsburgh were in close touch with the Shah's opponents and had been keeping the Administration informed. Even in Iran itself the opposition had been coming back to life and making people talk about it. The press was full of reports of the exploits of the Moujaheddin and Feddayin guerrillas (linked respectively with religious and Marxist circles).

Carter's error of judgment provides an ideal illustration of the great confusion reigning in America's information services. In September, just as the demonstrations were beginning to spread, the CIA had completed a report on the stability of the regime, finding that there was no domestic threat facing the Shah. On November 11, 1978, the President was to pass a harsh judgment, in writing, on those responsible in the State Department, the CIA and the National Security Council. It then emerged that, on the orders of their superiors, none of the agents of the various bodies working in Iran was allowed to criticize the regime or make contact with the opposition. Be that as it may, the absence of realistic evaluations of the situation in Iran goes some way toward explaining the hesitation of the American Administration throughout the events. Ignorance also accounts for the cautious line taken by the USSR and other countries which waited until the final weeks before withdrawing their support from the Shah.

Beginnings of the Crisis

In fact the crisis had been brewing for a long time. Since the election of Carter to the presidency, following a campaign which laid great stress on human rights, the Iranian opposition—encouraged by the example of the Soviet dissidents—had been organizing itself. Karim Sanjabi revived his National Front, the residue of the Mossadeq party of the 1950s, since gone dormant as a consequence of severe repression. The lawyer Lahidji and Mehdi Bazargan created a committee for the defense of human rights and liberties. Tracts and pamphlets circulated openly. Thus, in May 1977 more than

fifty lawyers signed a declaration protesting against interference by the executive in the affairs of the judiciary. In June a group of about forty writers called for
freedom of speech and the abolition of censorship. In
July some intellectuals addressed an open letter to the
Shah asking him to put an end to despotism. All kinds
of critical writings were circulating in secret. These activities marked a turning point in the political life of
the country, because the fact was that until then the
protests had occurred only abroad, or in the form of
attacks by urban guerrilla groups.

Meanwhile, under pressure from the United States,
the Shah launched a "liberalization" program. He tol-
erated a degree of criticism of his government in the
press and within the country's sole political party, Rastakhiz (Resurgence). He allowed a few deputies—still
party members—to vote against projects put forward
by the government. Although SAVAK maintained a
close watch on the various movements, it did not har-
ass the authors of the pamphlets and letters. The censorship, once paramount, was slightly eased. But these
timid changes did not quench the thirst for democracy
which was the driving force behind Iran's students and
intellectuals. Besides, nobody really believed in them.
Asked by the British journalist Alan Hart whether he
envisaged an English-style constitutional monarchy for
the future, the Shah replied to the effect that there was
no reason why not, if that was what the people wanted
—you could not rule people against their will, and if
that was what they wanted, then they would have it.*
Was he being sincere? I think so. He was attempting to
take over the idea of "democratization" launched by

* *The Times*, London, June 9, 1977.

the opposition, just as in 1960 he had appropriated the reforms advocated by the revolutionaries of that time. If they wanted revolution they'd get it, he used to say in those days, but they'd get it from him.

But in 1977 the opposition was on its guard. It saw his declarations as a performance put on to sidetrack Carter. In fact the freedom of debate promised to the press, and within the single Rastakhiz party, hung fire. And how could anybody ignore the sovereign's acid criticisms of Western democracy?

In his numerous interviews he never missed an opportunity to lay down the law to the great men of this world. He inveighed against the "permissive society" in the United States, the "idleness" of workers in England, the political "turmoil" in Italy, and so on. These admonitions also cropped up in his private conversation. In the summer of 1976 I found myself at the imperial table in Now Shahr, on the Caspian Sea, where a fellow guest was Marian Javits, wife of the senior Senator from New York and then a public-relations consultant to the Shah. An argument arose between the Shah and Mrs. Javits in which the sovereign severely criticized American democracy and asserted that Iranians enjoyed all conceivable human rights, and that corruption was unashamedly rampant in the United States, whereas in Iran the government arrested thieves even if they held high rank in society. The Shah's diatribe cast a chill over his guests.

Political activity was developing in the mosques, the traditional centers of opposition to the state. In a society where discontent finds no outlet in parliamentary institutions, the relative inviolability of the holy places makes them a natural focus of dissidence. Not only did the preachers mix social and political criticism with their preaching, but genuine debates ensued. Contraband recordings of Khomeini's speeches in Najaf were heard by large congregations, which spread the word outside the mosques. Travelers returning from Iraq were bringing back cassettes of Khomeini labeled as Oriental music to outwit customs and police checks. The tapes were on open sale in the shops of Qom and Tehran.

So, fifteen years after his exile, Khomeini's voice was heard throughout the land. On top of this, the Ayatollah was receiving visits in Najaf from all sorts of opponents of the regime. Thus, Yazdi and Ghotbzadeh (who were to become his right-hand men) saw him several times in 1977. All this was bound to infuriate the Shah, especially because the sermons of the exile in Najaf attacked him personally.

The Two Protagonists

The Shah detested Khomeini and made no secret of it. He lost no opportunity to belittle him—attentions which Khomeini returned with interest. Without harking back to the origin of their quarrel early in the 1960s, some more recent instances of their enmity may be cited. In 1971 the Shah told the correspondent of *Le Monde*, Eric Rouleau, "The Iranian people scorns a man like Khomeini, of foreign extraction, since he was born in India, and also a traitor to his adoptive country. It is even claimed that he is a paid agent of the British. He is also in the pay of Iraq."

This sally by the sovereign was made in retaliation against a lengthy attack delivered by Khomeini on the eve of the "celebrations" of the 2500th anniversary of the monarchy. In a speech whose printed text was forwarded to all the religious leaders of Iran, the exile in Najaf cried, "Are the Iranian people supposed to celebrate the man who betrayed Islam . . . the man who in 1963 . . . had a hundred people massacred in Qom and more than fifteen hundred in the whole country?"

And yet these two men who nursed such implacable hatred for each other are oddly alike. They are both stubborn and vindictive. They both advance simplistic ideas about the problems of their country and the world. Neither brooks any contradiction. Each considers himself guided by the Almighty. They want to be the undisputed leaders of the people. Their dictatorial spirit knows no bounds.

But, of course, they lead different lives. Khomeini is an ascetic, while the Shah compulsively surrounds himself with pomp and ceremony. "Given the historic, quasi-mystical side of the King and the significance of the monarchy for the people of Iran, no one here would understand any failure to observe certain rules in the presence of the sovereign," he confided to author Olivier Warin in 1975.*

Protocol aside, however, they echo each other. Listen to Khomeini: "From the religious point of view I am entitled to act as I do . . . When I saw the scale of the movement, I saw God in it. That cannot be the work of man." Then take the Shah, who once told some of his collaborators in my presence, "Without divine favor my revolution would not have been possible. Without

* Olivier Warin, *Le Lion et Le Soleil* (Paris: Éditions Stook, 1976).

God's support I would be a man like all the rest. And divine assistance will guarantee the continuation of our work."

In practice, Khomeini in power has been as intolerant as his predecessor. In a message to President Giscard d'Estaing he has deplored his "friends" in France "throwing human rights in his face over a few criminals and thieves."* The Shah for his part used to rail against those who brought in the issue of human rights to criticize him for his actions against "a few weeds." Of Marxists Khomeini says, "They are children who know nothing about Iranian society,"† and the Shah described them as "these people who at an adult age behave in a childish way." Khomeini, like the Shah, restricts the freedom of the press to news and articles which do not go counter to "popular feeling." Like SAVAK, the "Komiteh" makes arbitrary arrests and passes summary verdicts. Like the Shah's courts, the "Islamic" tribunals have ignored the rules of due process recognized throughout the Western world.

The truth is that the two men seem to have been cut out of the selfsame cloth.

Tehran, Sunday, January 8, 1978;
Qom, Monday, January 9, 1978

When he heard the reports about the smuggled cassettes, the Shah was furious with his secret services

* *Le Monde*, May 13–14, 1979.
† *Le Monde diplomatique*, April 1979.

and police. So far did his ill humor get the better of him that in his impatience to retaliate, and without consulting anybody, he ordered the publication of an article extremely damaging to the Ayatollah (the anonymous article accused him of homosexual leanings, made much of his foreign birth, alleged that his mother was a professional dancer, and so on). The Information Minister, Dariush Homayoun, Ardeshir Zahedi's brother-in-law, forced one of the big Tehran dailies to publish it. It was the spark which would touch off the powder keg.

The reaction was not long delayed. It erupted the very next day in Qom, the holy city which houses the tomb of Fatima. The faithful protested against the vile attacks directed against the religious leader by staging a demonstration around the mosque. Army and police opened fire on the crowd, and several people were killed.

There now began the series of mourning processions which by Iranian tradition are supposed to commemorate the departed on the fortieth day after their death. And since each new demonstration made new victims, every forty days the faithful had to brave the forces of order to venture onto the streets. The lay opposition made the most of these demonstrations. In increasing numbers they joined the religious marchers, swelling the ranks of the protesters. The Ayatollah Shariat-Madari (born in Tabriz and resident in Qom), who at seventy-six was the most respected religious leader in Iran, called on the faithful to protest against repression throughout the country.

The day after the events in Qom, Prime Minister Amuzegar stated before the Rastakhiz party's political bureau that the government's firm stand had forestalled the plans of traitors who were imperiling the nation's higher interests. In his view, the intervention of the forces of law and order had put a stop to the affair!

Nevertheless on February 18, 1978, in Tabriz, a procession some several thousand strong commemorated the victims of Qom. It turned into a riot, and according to eyewitnesses it was here that the first shouts of "Death to the Shah!" were heard. The crowd broke windows in banks and shops, and attacked the local offices of the Rastakhiz party—the banks because their practice of lending money at interest is contrary to the laws of Islam, the cinemas because they showed indecent films, the party because it represented the regime. The police fired into the crowd, and several people were killed. The government used its control of press and radio to minimize the affair, and as a sop to public feeling it replaced the governor of Azerbaijan and fired the Tabriz chief of police. As I look back on this period, what surprises me most is the Shah's misjudgment of the gravity of the situation. All the elements and all the actors in the crisis were gathered in Tabriz. He needed only to look, listen, and reflect.

On March 30, in response to a call from the religious leaders, marches were held in memory of the victims of Tabriz in several towns, most notably in Tehran and Esfahan. Once again the forces of order intervened. The authorities announced five deaths, the opposition more than thirty.

At this juncture political detainees in Tehran's Qasr prison went on a hunger strike. The government denied the news at first, but subsequently admitted it, trying at the same time to minimize its scale. The committee for the defense of human rights and liberties created by Bazargan accused the prison warders of mal-treating the strikers.

It came out later that demonstrations similar to the ones held in Tehran and Esfahan had occurred in other towns, many of them peaceful, as the religious leadership had advised. But in Yazd and in Jahrom, in the southeast of the country, they had given rise to violence. The government talked about three people killed in the two towns; the opposition put the figure at thirty-two.

That is how the vicious forty-day spiral which was to convulse the entire country was fueled, and how the contest became increasingly a religious revolution.

In Tehran a fairly unruffled Shah nevertheless criticized the head of SAVAK, General Nasiri, and his own Prime Minister. How had they allowed themselves to be overtaken by events? He ordered a counterdemonstration to be staged by the Rastakhiz party, and on April 2, the party leadership mustered up several thousand workers, peasants and notables in Tabriz.

I was then in Dakar in Senegal, where I listened to Radio Tehran's live transmission of the Tabriz meeting inside the Iranian Embassy. The assistant general secretary, Jafarian, addressed the crowd in a florid style far above the heads of the Tehran masses. He lauded the regime and the benefits of "the Revolution of the Shah and the People"—the peasants had become proprietors, the workers had a twenty percent stake in business profits, the people enjoyed social insurance, and so on. There were automatic bursts of applause each time the speaker pronounced the name of the sovereign. "This is lunacy!" I exclaimed. "Why?" asked the ambassador. I explained to him that the workers and peasants of Azerbaijan speak only the most elementary Persian. How on earth could they understand such a literary style? "The fact is," I told him, "that Jafarian isn't addressing the crowd, but the Shah, who is sure to be listening in on the radio." For this was common practice in the administration. Higher officials didn't give a damn about the impact of their statements on the people, only about the reaction of the Shah.

Unperturbed by the events in Tabriz, the sovereign continued to apply his policy of liberalization. But as usual his directives were far from clear. No one knew exactly what he had in mind and what limits he meant to set on freedom. The opposition saw the Shah's move as a trap: the authorities were trying to force dissidents to break cover. For their part the Shah's own men, habituated to long years of dictatorship, were also suspicious: they felt that the Shah wanted to put his supporters' loyalty to the test. This general skepticism was based on his previous constant criticism of democracy.

The Credibility of the Shah

In an interview granted on October 30, 1976, to the editor of the newspaper *Kayhan* the Shah declared:

> If democracy does exist, can it be different from what we are doing? . . . What is the true meaning of democracy?

For some it means attacking people, and particularly women, in broad daylight in the middle of towns and capitals, robbing them and then stabbing them. . . . And in countries where half the electorate abstains and where people are cut to pieces . . . there are those who criticize us on the subject of democracy and human rights. It's ludicrous. . . . What about the rights of those innocent people who are murdered in their homes, in the street or in a hotel room for money? Are they not human? Have they no rights? And if they have, who is going to protect them? And what do we do [in Iran]? We arrest people who are not only traitors but also terrorists. We protect our people against them and we do not offer them the chance of handing our country over to the enemy on a plate. Is that not protecting human rights? Who can claim that we do not protect human rights when we prevent the death of innocent people?

In his last book, with the resounding title of *Towards the Great Civilization*, published in Iran in 1977, he wrote:

In our democracy, individual liberty is inseparable from order and social discipline. Each citizen enjoys the fullest political, economic and social rights. . . . Ours is a democracy of legitimate liberties and legitimate political, economic and social rights, not of anarchy, sabotage or treason. By that I mean that in Iran we do not accept and do not pardon sabotage and disorder, and we refuse the rights of a citizen to those who have been duped, or who harbor evil intentions, as well as to lunatics, who in any case are in plentiful supply in the advanced countries and who unfortunately constitute a sort of terrorist international. These individuals who have been led astray by ignorance or illogicality, or by brainwashing, or again as a consequence of a mental aberration, in the name of incoherent ideologies such as Islamic Marxism (whose innate contradiction even a child could grasp), are performing acts of sabotage and even murder against their country, and naturally to the advantage of foreign interests, in the belief that sowing disorder is part of their "heroic" mission. Obviously the activities of these individuals, whether they are simply stupid or deliberately treasonous, are without consequence when up against the vigor of the progressive, constructive order of the country, and cannot give rise to any real worries. But it is annoying to see these few weeds rearing their heads, like those people who at an adult age behave in a childish way.

My Last Encounter with the Shah

My last meeting with the Shah was in April 1978.

In the anteroom there was a discussion going on among a number of lavishly gold-braided and bemedaled military men. They were quite undisturbed by the events in Qom, Tabriz, Esfahan and Yazd as they chatted about the various sections of the Army under their command. I was astonished to observe that the Shah was receiving them one at a time. The last man to enter the imperial office, the chief of staff, was not at all offended by what was, to say the least, an unusual procedure. It was often said that the Shah approved of the idea of divide and rule, but who would have thought to such an extent?

Finally it was my turn. I found the Shah determined to pursue his policy of "liberalization." As usual he hardly let me get a word in edgeways, talking and talking as if delivering a speech to himself. He painted an optimistic picture of the country and its progress. "We have beaten inflation," he claimed. (Certainly the prices of foodstuffs were set at a reasonable level, but these were available only on the black market.) Then he brought up the question of the recent disturbances: "It's nothing. Tabriz? Esfahan? It's the price to be paid for democratization. Nothing dangerous. And then who can oppose me? Khomeini? He doesn't count for much. Sanjabi and the rest? They are incompetents, and often traitors." When I blanched at these remarks, he looked me in the eye. "Yes—we have documents which establish their connections, like Mossadeq's connections, with their foreign masters."

Here I managed to squeeze a question in: "If these proofs exist, why do you not publish them?"

"When the time is right," he replied. He took a sip of tea and resumed. "All these people are afraid of my policy of liberalization, just as they feared my policy of reforms in 1962. It cuts the ground from under their feet. They don't frighten me. I shall continue to go forward. The people, the true people, are with me."

I felt him out on the subject of his book *Towards the Great Civilization* (which I had just translated into French on his orders, with the help of my colleague Soheyla Shahkar), to try to make him understand the negative responses it was bound to produce. But it was time wasted: the "great civilization" was his hobby-horse, his very own little invention, an imaginary world which was more real to him than reality. He interrupted me in midsentence to say, "Everybody is saying nothing but good about it. What I develop in this book is crucially important for the country's future."

In the thirty-seven years of his reign he never understood the danger of flattery. The book's English translator, Fouad Rouhani, agreed with Soheyla Shahkar and me that it was an outburst of delirium, if not paranoia. It was not so much the reactions it was certain to provoke that worried us, but its content. The Shah's book described an idyllic national situation which was nowhere to be found:

> Our revolution, which started fifteen years ago, constitutes the greatest change in the history of Iran. . . . Through it, all barriers to positive action have been removed, thus allowing the free flowering of all talents and potentialities, as well as the Iranian people's equitable enjoyment of the product of their labour. . . .
>
> Today our economy, founded upon realism and foresight, is growing daily more sound, and thanks to that a new Iran is being born, benefiting all its citizens. . . .
>
> When it comes to halting inflation, ours is an unbeaten and unprecedented record in the world. . . .
>
> In recent years our society has come to enjoy numerous privileges with no great difficulty. . . . Some advantages granted to the workers in Iran are unequalled even in the most advanced industrialized countries and the socialist world. Similarly the rights and privileges of the peasants of Iran are far ahead of those which it has taken agricultural workers in many countries centuries to acquire. . . . In the field of general social welfare the industrialized countries, despite their long and difficult struggle, are outstripped by Iran.

I could give more examples, but these few excerpts are enough to show the divorce between the thinking of the Shah and the facts of everyday life.

In Senegal, before returning to Tehran, I had spoken to Sadruddin Aga Khan and Andrew Young, the American ambassador to the UN, and told them, "It's unbelievable. He is completely losing touch with reality. If you want my opinion there's trouble on the way. It can't go on." Talking to officials in Tehran, I could tell that they had hardly so much as leafed through the book. Yet the Shah continued his soliloquy: "Liberalization is necessary. We are entering a new phase of our revolution. After all, Juan Carlos has managed it, and there were a few hitches there too . . ."

As I left the palace I took with me a feeling of deep pessimism. No one dared tell him that you can't be Franco and Juan Carlos at the same time. And what I had been fearing for a long time was now confirmed: he was out of touch with reality and did not realize the extent of the unrest in his country. Not since the 1950s, I reflected, had Iran seemed to me to be in such a state of discontent as in that spring of 1978. Wherever I went, friends and strangers alike made no bones about expressing their criticisms. Power cuts, food shortages, galloping inflation (in spite of the government's victory bulletins), exorbitant rents, traffic jams, censorship, repression—all this and more was boiling up and getting ready to blow the lid off. And if people were not yet openly insulting the monarch himself, they were certainly complaining about his family: Abdorreza has done this, Gholamreza has done that, and so on, dropping their royal titles. But the favorite target was the Shah's twin sister, Princess Ashraf. Returning from the casino in Cannes in 1977, her car had run into an ambush, and various versions of the incident were being retailed in Tehran in spring 1978: that there was an involvement with a drug ring, or that it had been a Mafia attack. The names of the people with her were common knowledge, and that she and her entourage monopolized most of the country's business was a common belief.

My Last Meetings with My Brother

I dined with my brother (who then held the post of minister of the court), and he agreed with me that the image of the Shah as "father" of the nation was definitely moribund and that discontent was rife. "The royal family carries a heavy responsibility in all this," Amir Abbas said. "If the Shah loses his throne it will be because of his brothers and sisters. You cannot know what the court is like: a rat race, and a hive of corruption. I have talked to the Boss about it. [He had called the Shah by this name ever since joining the government.] I have told him a thousand times that when it comes to fighting corruption true charity begins at home, and he should deal rigorously with his own. In 1975, when the American Senate inquiry disclosed that millions of dollars in commissions had gone to people in high places here, including members of his own family, he told me that it was only natural, that his brothers and sisters had the right to do business and to earn their living like everybody else, and that the practice of business commissions was common everywhere."

I said to my brother that this was a good demonstration of the Shah's inability to understand the distinction between payment for services rendered and downright theft.

"Yes," said my brother, "but he eventually gave in to my arguments and authorized me to draw up a code of conduct for the royal family. By the terms of this code they will have no right to participate in any business dealings where the state is involved. They will not be allowed to recommend people to ministers, or to ask ministers for favors. They will no longer be able to hold official posts, and so on. Unfortunately, every time I ask him to publish the code, he tells me to wait."

This code was not officially revealed until the end of October, when most of the princes and princesses were already out of the country. Be that as it may, I found my brother pessimistic by comparison with the year before. A few days later, at a reception attended by some members of the royal family, I saw him gesture toward the conspicuous display of the whole gathering and heard him whisper in a friend's ear, "We're living in the last days of Pompeii."

Before leaving Tehran I went to see my brother again, and asked him why he did not resign. "I've come this far," he said. "I don't want to leave the ship now that the storm is brewing. Really I ought to have gone in 1974, after the oil boom. It was after that that everything changed."

"And what if I left the Foreign Ministry?" I asked him. "Would that bother you?"

"No, why should it? Do as you wish. But in the present situation, what will your gesture prove? People will distrust you on both sides, left as well as right. They'll

say that you ran out when you saw trouble coming."
He lit his pipe, puffed on it, then went on to say, "You
have to help to settle these problems. Our country is at
stake. You remember your friends on the left. If I was
not here and you had not warned me, a lot of them
would now be under the ground. I have always tried to
keep the temperature down and to help the men of the
people, and the clergy. . . . And if I left my job, the
profiteers would steal even more."

I told Amir Abbas that I no longer had any confidence in the Shah. "His book is dreadful. What a difference from 1965. He is no longer the same man. You'll
see, he'll abandon ship and leave us all. You should
have got out in 1975 when you were ill and when all
those corruption scandals broke out."

My brother cleaned out the bowl of his pipe. "We're
all living under the same regime, and we cooperate
whether we like it or not. Those who are in government
and those who are not. And there isn't any choice. In
this country you can't resign. You have to not get involved in the first place."

"What about the responsibilities?" I insisted.

"What responsibilities?" My brother sounded irritated. "He makes the decisions himself. I don't even
know what is happening in the Army and SAVAK.
. . . I try to do my best. I have never stolen a penny. I
have never given orders to fire into the crowd . . ."

My brother was to repeat many of these words at the
time of the mockery of a trial to which he was subjected
early in April 1979. And after his murder Mehdi Bazargan, Khomeini's Prime Minister, echoed them almost
verbatim. Just like Amir Abbas, he was to tender his
resignation several times, and have it refused. Why

does he stay at his post in spite of the difficulties created for him by the existence of other centers of power? Is it not because, like my brother, he is thinking of the national interest? Is is not because he believes that if he gives up his job, his successors will become even more extreme? Does he not imagine that his presence will cushion a good many shocks? It is worth bearing in mind the similarity between the two situations.

When I said farewell to my brother I did not know that I would never see him again.

Relative Calm Descends

In Qom on May 10, 1978, the security forces pursued "rioters" into the supposedly inviolable houses of various religious leaders, in particular Ayatollah Shariat-Madari. The government issued a communiqué in which it "deeply regretted" the incident: "The fact that rioters acting against the national interest were pursued [into certain houses] is explained by the ignorance of agents who were not natives of Qom." Nevertheless there were still numerous arrests made all over the country.

On May 11 a demonstration in Tehran backed by the religious leaders forced the Shah to postpone a trip abroad and to take command of the Army in order to avoid "a useless bloodbath." On the sixteenth the sovereign stated that he intended to pursue his policy of "liberalization," but that the Army would not sit still in face of "provocations whose ultimate objective is to partition the country." On June 5 the bazaars in Tehran, Mashad, Qom and Tabriz shut down.

In order to gain a degree of credibility for his efforts toward democratization, the sovereign dismissed Nasiri from the SAVAK leadership and appointed him ambassador to Pakistan. This is a convenient place to point out one noteworthy feature of the regime: that its decisions were always ambiguous. If the Shah genuinely wanted to repudiate the behavior of his secret police he should have had Nasiri put to trial. He did not do so until November, but by then it would be too late. From then on, all the measures taken by the Shah and his government became ineffective. They appeared to be either timid or dictated by events. In replacing Nasiri by a more moderate man, General Moghadam, the Shah tried to mollify public resentment, but the people thought that the violent reactions of the police were sheer provocations intended to create a climate of terror and thereby deter demonstrations.

Nevertheless, the meeting held on June 17, 1978, in memory of those killed at Qom passed without incident. While the Tehran bazaar and a few shops stayed shut that day, there was business as usual elsewhere. And the police confined themselves to breaking up any gatherings around the mosques.

From his lair in Najaf, Khomeini declared that the recent riots constituted the first rumblings of a "gigantic explosion." The Shah was unmoved. He informed the correspondent of *U.S. News and World Report* (June 26, 1978) that the demonstrations amounted in some cases to acts of personal vengeance against himself. He ascribed the opposition of certain religious leaders to his modernization program, denounced the "strange phenomenon" of Communists working with Muslims, and coolly asserted, "Nobody can overthrow me. I have the support of 700,000 troops, all the workers and most of the people." He rejected the idea of a regime comprising several political parties and claimed that many political prisoners had been released and that the rest would be if they agreed to "repent." But he was no longer talking in terms of a period of five years to make Iran an industrialized country. "In ten years, we hope to be what Europe is today. It will not be easy, but in twenty years we hope to be a fully advanced nation." He credited his policy of "liberalization" with the reduction of acts of "terrorism," when the fact is that the severely decimated urban guerrilla groups were taking time off to get their breath back and reorganize for more decisive battles. They were making contact with Khomeini and the refugee opposition in Europe.

Obviously the Shah had hardly shifted his position at all in relation to most of the country's problems. Late that June he still had no inkling of the deep-seated nature of the disease and the gravity of the situation. How was this possible, coming from a man who had shown such flair on other occasions?

Actually he has only himself to blame. Over the years his dictatorial cast of mind had discouraged criticism and contradiction. For fear of annoying him, his collaborators—even the agents of SAVAK—watered down their reports. If he had been open to the realities, and if he had paid attention to some of his advisers (my brother among them), he might conceivably have managed to stage a recovery by acting on three fronts: he should have declared open warfare against corruption, starting with his own family; granted freedom of expression and dissolved the single Rastakhiz party, whose lack of popular roots was only too plain; and negotiated with Ayatollah Shariat-Madari and other moderate religious leaders. In fact Khomeini did not then occupy his subsequent position as undisputed leader of the opposition. The moderate religious leaders were not asking for the abolition of the monarchy but for the application of the Constitution of 1906 and respect for religion by the state.

Instead of taking advantage of the relative calm of the month of July to mount some decisive action and open a dialogue with the religious and lay opposition, the Shah went off on his annual vacation by the Caspian Sea with his friends ex-King Constantine of Greece and King Hussein of Jordan.

Khomeini himself did not rest. He redoubled his recorded sermons and strengthened his links with Iran's religious centers and his new supporters abroad. (Yazdi had established and reinforced his Islamic movement in the United States, and Ghotbzadeh was in touch with the Palestine Liberation Organization.) He was already determined to secure the maximum advantage from the movement which had begun in Iran. The lay opposition was organizing, too, and intellectuals were running off mimeographed sheets which went into underground circulation. The young felt lost in a consumer society which could offer them no comfort or morality. Corruption was rife, and there were only newspaper articles and flowery speeches to oppose it. The Rastakhiz party was lost in a tangle of contradictions. To the two existing camps a third was now added, under the control of Houshang Nahavandi, former rector of Tehran University, former Cabinet minister, and the Empress's private secretary. Internal struggles were going on within the party, and its general secretary, Prime Minister Amuzegar, intended using them solely for his own advantage.

On August 5, in a message broadcast on the occasion of the anniversary of the constitution, the Shah promised "one hundred percent free elections" for June 1979. Candidates not belonging to the Rastakhiz party would be allowed to stand under the designation of their choice. Only the Communists, "forbidden by law," would be excluded. The news was greeted with skepticism.

While the opposition to the regime was daily drawing closer together under the banner of religion, inside the ruling class the divisions were widening. Sensing the imminent fall of the Amuzegar government, under which the security forces had killed hundreds of people since January, the likely ministerial appointees were prepared. Nahavandi, who enjoyed the confidence of the Empress, had some of the younger men behind him. Ardeshir Zahedi, who had always wanted to become prime minister, recalled himself to his friends' attention. Among the "old establishment," Ali Amini, a former prime minister, was renewing his contacts with clerical circles. The rumor mill ground on. Some people talked about a possible comeback by my brother, thereby paying tribute to his fundamental honesty and "political flexibility." This latter possibility upset the other candidates, who united to plant attacks on my brother in the gutter press. Besides that, since his appointment as prime minister Amuzegar had often criticized the government's actions of the previous fourteen years, forgetting that he himself had belonged to it. And knowing the absence of free speech, how could anyone believe that the slanders spread about my brother were spontaneous?

I telephoned Amir Abbas to ask him why he did not reply—wasn't he afraid that his silence would be misinterpreted? His answer was that the Shah did not like his Minister of the Court to get involved in squabbles with the press. Friends told me that the sovereign found the situation convenient: himself under personal attack by the opposition, he hoped to divert criticism onto his collaborators.

Looking back on that period, I cannot prevent myself from asking a number of disturbing questions. Was it not the Shah himself who inspired the whole campaign? Ever since my brother's dismissal as prime minister in August 1977 he had allowed his present Prime Minister, various deputies and a section of the press to go on reiterating false allegations against Amir Abbas. Perhaps he was already thinking of making him the scapegoat for his own mistakes?

The New Wave of Violence

It was in this atmosphere of uncertainty that violence broke out in Esfahan on August 11, 1978, on the occasion of the beginning of the month of Ramadan. From daybreak onward hundreds of people, most of them young and armed with cans of gasoline, invaded the town center and burned police vehicles, banks and cinemas, to cries of *"Shah haroumzadch!"* (Shah bastard). The police and the Army opened fire with automatic weapons, claiming more than a hundred victims.

Why this sudden explosion of violence? The previous day, people had been taking turns at the house of a religious dignitary to protest against the arrest of another priest. The police had assaulted and shot at them, thereby antagonizing the whole town. The most fantastic rumors were spread, alleging that Israeli commandos disguised as Iranian soldiers were responsible for the shooting. On the orders of the Shah, the government imposed a state of siege, but the populace defied the curfew, and strikes and demonstrations broke out all over the country, in Yazd, Tabriz, Shiraz, Qom, Tehran and elsewhere. Groups of young men attacked anything which remotely represented the regime—police and Army vehicles, the offices of foreign companies, Rastakhiz party meeting rooms, and so on. SAVAK was accused of street killings carried out by plainclothesmen, and there were reports of anonymous phone calls threatening members of the opposition.

It was at this point that, on the evening of August 19, fire gutted the Rex cinema in Abadan, taking a toll of 377 victims according to official figures. The government press and radio first blamed this "criminal" act on a group of religious fanatics, and then on foreign agents. Feelings ran very high. When Amuzegar heard the news he gave orders for an immediate inquiry. The opposition accused the police and SAVAK thugs.

On Tuesday, August 22, thousands of people lamented over the newly dug graves in the cemetery at Abadan. The crowd poured out into the streets, to shouts of "Death to provocateurs!" The investigations were making no headway, and rumors multiplied. The fire brigade of this oil town was one of the best equipped in the country; why had it taken so long to arrive? There was talk that the police had failed to alert them until half an hour after the outbreak, that the cinema exits had been locked, that agents had prevented volunteers from trying to help the trapped audience, and so on.

After a first rash of articles blaming the incident on extremists, the press fell mysteriously silent. The government kept silent, too. Two weeks after the event it was announced that the Iraqi authorities had arrested one of the men responsible at the frontier. The culprit was handed over to the Iranian police and underwent interrogation, but then silence descended again. The affair remains a mystery to this day. Nobody knows, and probably no one will ever know, who started the fire. That being so, the provocation theory appears the most likely.

Following a hurried return to Iran, the Shah showed the first signs of apprehension. In interviews given to the foreign press he repeated his commitment to liberalization, made overtures to the opposition, issued some vehement warnings and promised free elections.

On Wednesday, August 23, the Tehran vegetable market, set afire by "terrorists," burned down. Newspaper editorials called for conciliation. The liberal opposition ignored the proffered hand. Karim Sanjabi, president of the National Front, held a press conference and condemned "the government's policy of terror, and its empty promises."

Khomeini, whose star was still on the rise, called for

disobedience by soldiers and police: "Do not obey orders which require you to kill unjustly." His calls for an uprising to overthrow the Shah now had more repercussions in the superheated atmosphere than the less violent appeals of the other ayatollahs. For the first time the exile in Najaf spoke of an Islamic republic.

In that late August the longing to get rid of the Shah was smoldering in various areas of the population— among the mullahs, the tradesmen in the bazaars and some members of the middle classes as well as in the universities and various Marxist groups, pro-Soviet or not. But because they were pursuing different objectives they lacked a focal center. Khomeini and his appeal to Islamic fervor was to provide it. His person became the cement of the rebellion.

How is such a development to be explained? It cannot be done without considering the influence, even upon Iranians brought up on the Western pattern, of Shi'ism, the official religion of Iran since the sixteenth century. There is a story that on the occasion of the Tehran demonstration in September 1978, Sanjabi, the leader of the National Front, said, "I am no longer myself but an ourself among others, a Muslim among others."* I myself felt this quasi-mystical fervor in 1958, at the Tehran bazaar, while filming the procession on the day of Ashura in memory of the martyrdom of the Imam Hussein. Overcome with emotion, I abandoned my camera to a foreign friend and mingled my sighs with the crowd's. I do not intend to give an account of Shi'ism, the religion of ninety-five percent of my fellow countrymen, but I do think it necessary to point out

* Quoted in Claire Brière and Pierre Blanchet, *Iran, la révolution au nom de dieu* (Paris: Éditions du Seuil, 1979).

certain aspects of the Shi'ite faith which go some way toward explaining the events which led to the Shah's inexorable downfall.

While Shi'ism professes, like Sunnism, that Moham-mad was the "Seal of the Prophecy," the last Prophet, it holds that the final point of the "cycle of the proph-ecy" coincides with the initial point of the "cycle of the imams," who are seen as the custodians of the "secret of the emissary of God." The twelve imams are those who guide their followers on the esoteric spiritual way of the Revelation announced by the Prophet. The first, Ali, the husband of Fatima, daughter of the Prophet, was stabbed to death in 661. His two sons Hassan and Hussein were also assassinated. The period of the holy imams goes up to the "great occultation" in 940 of the twelfth imam, Mohammad àl Ghaim, who is to return at the end of time. There then begins the secret history of the hidden imam, which makes Shi'ism into the es-oteric branch of Islam. The Shi'ites are those who as-sume the secrets of the imams and conserve the hidden meaning of the Book. It is precisely the secrecy and mysticism which it has developed in Iran that exercise such a powerful attraction. Shi'ism has survived down the centuries, through the advent of the Safavids and through all persecution, thanks to the conviction of the faithful that they are the witnesses of the true Islam. What is at stake for them is the safeguarding of the spiritual against all the perils of the temporal.

The history of Iran and the Shi'ite tradition are closely intertwined and have never ceased to develop in the course of the centuries. The eighty thousand or so mosques and the 180,000 mullahs constitute a well-organized infrastructure capable of mobilizing the masses whenever necessary against anything seen by the guides, the ayatollahs, as a source of persecution. All through 1978 the Shah came more and more to personify corruption and repression in the eyes of the faithful. This explains the religious complexion worn by the Iranian revolutionary movement. Add to this the teaching of a man like Ali Shariati, professor of sociology at the University of Mashhad, which gives Shi'ism a modern social content, and the reader will understand the majority of students rallying to Khomeini's watchword. Ali Shariati died in exile in London. The faithful accused SAVAK immediately, and made him a martyr. To anyone familiar with the key role of the martyrdom of Imam Hussein in the Iranian tradition, Shariati's influence becomes clear. The same factor explains the crucial part played by those processions in memory of the demonstration victims, which from one forty-day period to the next were to transform the original protest movement into a genuine revolution.

The Shah Faces the Facts

With the persistence of the disorders and the approach of the Eidé Fetr, which marks the end of the month's fasting of Ramadan, the Shah sensed that Amuzegar was not the man for the situation. Since January he had been unable either to galvanize the Rastakhiz party into the necessary action or to reduce the level of reli-

gious agitation. Instead he had caused considerable resentment not only in the opposition but among the
regime's own supporters. The circumstances required
not a technocrat but an experienced politician who
knew also how to appeal to the mullahs. The Shah followed what had now become his customary course of
talking to the American ambassador, who apparently
mentioned my brother. The idea was rejected. From
that moment onward, prompted by circles connected
with various members of his own family (damaged by
the fight against corruption) and with Ardeshir Zahedi
(motivated by his personal animosity), he decided to
discard Amir Abbas. The American ambassador later
told a mutual friend, who passed it on to me, "The
Shah is jealous of Hoveyda. Yet he's one of the few
political brains in the country."

Be that as it may, the Shah ordered Amuzegar to
resign and instructed the President of the Senate, Jaafar
Sharif-Emami, to form a new Cabinet. At the same
time, in an attempt to create the impression of a genuine change of direction, he dismissed most of his former colleagues from their posts, my brother among
them. That day a friend passing through New York told
me, "I think it's the end of the King." Seeing my surprise, he reminded me of a dinner given by Princess
Fatmeh in 1973, when the sovereign had turned to
Amir Abbas and publicly proclaimed, "I think that we
shall take our retirement together, you and I!"

In fact this action was one of the miscalculations
which he was to keep on making during the last
months of his reign, by which I do not mean that he
had forgotten his prophecy! Because not only was he
creating a vacuum around himself, but Sharif-Emami,

although he belonged to a family which had produced some important religious figures, had for some time directed the Pahlavi Foundation, which public opinion considered a center for the royal family's illegal profiteering. In most circles he was regarded as corrupt.

Before even announcing his Cabinet team, Sharif-Emami announced with a flourish the closing of Iran's casinos (gambling is forbidden by Islam), the return to the calendar of the Hegira—the Prophet's flight from Mecca to Medina (a year previously the Shah had put it back to the foundation of the Persian Empire by Cyrus) —and the abolition of the Women's Ministry instituted at the request of the Shah's twin sister. He also allowed the press to publish pictures of Khomeini. He thereby demonstrated, just as the Shah did, his ignorance of the deep-seated nature of the crisis. In fact these cosmetic measures did not deceive anyone. Khomeini was already demanding the removal of the Shah and the institution of an Islamic republic. The moderate clergy in Iran were calling for the strict application of the Constitution of 1906, notably the provision giving five of them a right of veto over any law judged contrary to the principles of Islam. As for the intellectuals and the eighteen or so parties which had suddenly sprung up, they were demanding total freedom.

In Tehran some circles were looking toward the United States, which had kept quiet until then. The CIA had orchestrated General Zahedi's *coup d'état* against Mossadeq in 1953; would it intervene again to support the Shah? Rumors spread faster still when the General's son Ardeshir, Iran's ambassador in Washington, suddenly became active on the political scene. He boasted of having been instrumental in the change of government, and told anyone willing to listen that he had chosen several of the new ministers, including the Foreign Office appointee, Amir Khosrow Afshar.

In the absence of the liberal opposition, which still refused all contact with him, the Shah called in for consultation the representatives of the "old establishment" whom he had removed from power in 1963: Ali Amini, Abdollah Entezam, and the rest. Thus he almost entirely cut himself off from those who had worked with him for the past fifteen years. He redoubled his contacts with the American and British ambassadors, with a view to ensuring the support of the West, and received frequent visits from his army chiefs.

According to confidential information I received at that time, the Shah was steering between two opposing currents. On one side were the supporters of conciliation and concessions to the clergy, represented by Sharif-Emami and the "old establishment"; on the other side the army hardliners, all for a policy of force. Obviously he was not prepared to listen to the "liberals" (the National Front, the intellectuals and others) who were demanding his abdication and a return to the constitution. Throughout the following months he was to hover between these two poles. And day by day under the pressure of events he was slowly to lose his self-assurance. His face grew haggard, his eyes glassy, his voice shaky. Returning from a visit to Iran, Michael Blumenthal, American secretary of the treasury, said (according to a friend who passed it on to me), "He is not functioning." Calling in Sharif-Emami was a serious mistake, as events were soon to prove.

How are we to explain the Shah's vacillation in face of the worsening crisis? The truth is that, outpaced by the concessions which he himself allowed his own Prime Minister to grant, weakened by months of civil unrest, and cut off from his usual advisers, he felt the need for solid backing, and went looking for it among his Western friends. A court acquaintance informed me later that the sovereign often complained that "the Americans" would not give him a free hand to settle the crisis in his own way. So, where immediate surgery was required, the Shah used first aid. Not only did he fail to meet the expectations of the opposition but he also displeased his own troops, among whom discord had already set in.

At that stage in the sequence of events there was only one course open to him, that of humility and self-criticism. By publicly admitting his mistakes, explaining his motivation, choosing ministers from among the people and getting rid of sycophants, thieves and fools, he could have stayed. But with his rigid character and limitless pride it was not possible for him to take that course. Possible or not, however, far from lowering the temperature, the arrival of Sharif-Emami on the scene raised it to boiling point.

The Violence Resumes

On Monday, September 4, the Eidé Fetr ended the month of Ramadan and provided the occasion for a demonstration by the people of Tehran. A vast crowd flooded into the streets chanting slogans against the

Shah after having first gathered in the Gaytarieh quarter—a large area of waste ground—to pray. The liberal opposition joined the Muslim faithful in this religious expression of the popular will. In the march that followed, the first cries of "Long live Khomeini" went up, and when the human tide met trucks crammed with armed soldiers the marchers threw flowers to the soldiers and called out, "Brothers, don't shoot." Some of the soldiers were moved to tears, and the procession was allowed to proceed.

On September 7 the people of Tehran took to the streets again, despite the counsels of caution. And the chanted slogans became more and more pointed: "Death to the Shah!" "Long live Khomeini!" "Our religion is Musseini, our Shah is Khomeini." "Shah without honor, get out." "Fifty years of reign, fifty years of treason." "Shah, we'll kill you." "Soldiers, our brothers, join us." The huge procession wound on. It was only by a miracle that a bloody confrontation was avoided.

In less than two months (July and August) Khomeini's hold on the crowd was an established fact. The exile in Najaf was stronger than the ayatollahs in Iran. He became the sole and undisputed leader of the movement that had started nine months earlier.

The military were alarmed at the turn of events. "We must have martial law," they insisted to the Shah. "Today the crowd could have taken control of Parliament and the radio and television stations." After a great deal of hesitation and consultations with the American and British ambassadors, the Shah eventually agreed. He sensed that his liberalization policy was crumbling. Not that this worried the military.

They had been critical of it in private for a long time. To this day some of them attribute the fall of the regime to that policy and to Carter's insistence on human rights.

In the small hours of the morning of Friday, September 8, a government communiqué concerning the previous day's demonstration was broadcast over the radio, announcing:

> This demonstration, organized against the advice of religious leaders, was aimed against the state and the constitution and was tolerated only out of the concern not to shed blood unnecessarily. . . . Considering as it does that the ramifications of the plot, planned and financed by outside forces, are spreading and endangering the individual rights, liberty and independence of the Nation, and that they are directed toward putting an end to Iran's march forward, the government, which is responsible for the proper application of the constitution, decrees martial law for a period of six months.

General Ali Oveissi, formerly the commander of the Imperial Guard, and a hawk, became the administrator of martial law.

Many people in Tehran did not hear the radio that morning. (Even General Jafari, the deputy chief of police, admitted that he had not been informed of the new measure.) They therefore did as they had agreed the previous day and headed for Jaleh Square, where on September 1 the police and the Army had opened fire on worshipers who shouted slogans as they emerged from the Fatima Mosque. Submachine guns opened up on the demonstrators, most of them young, and there was talk of a deliberate massacre. According to the government the death toll came to fifty-eight; according to the opposition, five hundred. Throughout the day sporadic bursts of gunfire were heard in various parts of the capital.

Tehran's "Black Friday" was to denote an irreversible turning point. The wildest rumors circulated, among them that three planeloads of Israeli commandos had arrived the previous day to carry out the squalid task which Iranian soldiers had refused to accept.

Feeling ran high in opposition circles, where it was felt that the United States would never have given the green light to the Shah. Many opponents went underground. Many others, including religious leaders, were arrested. Shahpur Bakhtiar, the vice-president of the National Front (who later agreed to become the Shah's last prime minister), told the correspondent of *Le Monde*, "There is no longer any possibility of compromise with the regime."

Next day Khomeini launched an appeal for "resistance to the criminal Shah" and asked the Army to rebel. For his part the sovereign declared in an interview in *Time* magazine that had it not been for martial law his opponents might have taken control of the country. At last the highly respected Ayatollah Shariat-Madari proclaimed a state of national mourning to be observed with calm and dignity.

On Sunday, September 10, Sharif-Emami presented his government to Parliament, under the protection of the tanks. He stated that the process of liberalization would continue, that he intended to create a calm atmosphere for holding free elections and to get rid of corruption.

Meanwhile the stricken families were furtively burying their dead in the cemetery of Behechté Zahra ("the Paradise of Zahra").

On the same day Sharif-Emami called for the princes and princesses of the royal family to close down their business offices, while the Shah gave a garden party for 120 bankers representing international high finance, who were visiting Iran to celebrate the fiftieth birthday of the National Bank.

That same day, in Washington, a panic-stricken Zahedi, thinking that he was acting for the best, telephoned President Carter's national-security adviser, Zbigniew Brzezinski, at Camp David and begged him to work on the President. Between meetings with Egyptian President Sadat and Israeli Prime Minister Begin, Carter made a phone call to the Shah to assure him of his support. This call, like the President's statements during the following months, far from helping the Shah stirred up still more anger and contempt against him.

Concerning the situation at that moment, Ali Amini, the former prime minister of the 1960s who was attempting a political comeback, subsequently told the special correspondent of Le Monde, "I have always supported the regime, and it was my intention to build a bridge between His Majesty and the opposition. . . . It is true that the Shah did not make my task any easier. . . . In the event of his agreeing to reign, but no more than that, I would have formed a government of national unity and organized free elections." There was a lot of talk in and after September of the "Amini solution," but I do not see how he could have surmounted the twin obstacles of Khomeini and the objections from the left. He was seen as being in the pocket of the

Americans, and could not have counteracted the anti-American feelings which were already developing.*

Nevertheless, in the days that followed, the government opened its promised campaign against corruption, except that instead of tackling the "big names" in the Shah's entourage, which might have had a favorable impact on public opinion, Sharif-Emami contented himself with putting a few scapegoats out to pasture. He arrested a former Minister of Health, for example. The top people got the message at once, and made a stealthy exit from the scene, taking with them everything they had not yet shipped out of the country. The Shah continued his endless series of interviews with the foreign press—interviews which simply gave ammunition to his opponents. (I have never understood the sudden propensity for ranting which took hold of him after the quadrupling of the price of oil. Everybody who interviewed him said that he was his own worst enemy, not only because of what he said, but because of his harsh and forbidding appearance on television.) He continued to blame "Communists" and "anarchists" for his difficulties.

Thinking that he was still in the 1950s and 1960s, Sharif-Emami embarked on a strategy of promises and concessions to reduce the pressure. His version of the stick-and-carrot policy was intended to divide the opposition, as for example when he released the more moderate detainees of Black Friday and kept the mili-

* On the eve of the Shah's visit to the United States in November 1977, Arnaud de Borchgrave of *Newsweek* asked the sovereign, "Your government released a news report two weeks ago alleging that President Kennedy in 1961 used $35 million in U.S. aid to pressure you into appointing Dr. Ali Amini as prime minister. Is the report correct?" The Shah replied, "It's past history but correct."

tants in jail. Quite clearly, he did not realize the scope and nature of the unrest. He had barely taken power when he allowed himself to be overtaken by events.

The situation was going from bad to worse. At one point, after the devastating earthquake in Khorasan, it looked as if things might quiet down a little, but they did not. When we tuned in to Radio Tehran in the office, its news bulletin started as usual: "Today Her Majesty the Shahbanou put Madame Farideh Diba [her mother] in charge of coordinating rescue operations . . ." One of my colleagues shrugged his shoulders. "Same old story. They'll never learn. They'll never change." And in fact it has to be acknowledged that the radio news bulletins always angered the listeners; they invariably started with a detailed account of the doings of the royal family, even when important news was pouring out of the teletype machines.

The Strikes

With the ban on demonstrations, and the Army keeping watch, the struggle against the regime assumed new forms. On days of mourning the tradesmen in the bazaars and the small shopkeepers put up their shutters. The workers' response was to start wielding the strike weapon, and this truly unsettled the Shah, who believed in their loyalty. (These were the same workers who in January 1976 expressed their "eternal gratitude" to the Shahanshah when receiving from the imperial hand shares in the enterprises where they worked for the Shah.)

The stoppages began as purely economic moves. The government held talks with strikers in the public sector and granted pay raises, some of them as high as forty percent. The heads of private industries were officially encouraged to follow suit.

Meanwhile, in answer to representations from the Iranian government, and following Khomeini's calls for rebellion, Iraq took restrictive measures against the Ayatollah. Basing their case on the fact that the exiled Khomeini was a kind of political refugee, the Iraqis forbade him to have any contacts with visitors from Iran. These isolation measures led to protests. The opposition in Iran called a general strike for Sunday, October 1, which was widely observed in Tehran and the main provincial towns. The Iranian Foreign Minister had been in New York attending the General Assembly of the United Nations; he pursued his negotiations with his Iraqi colleague and managed to get Khomeini expelled.

In a gesture of reconciliation the government announced that all Iranians abroad might come home on the sole condition that they "respect the constitution." This amounted to an amnesty for students hostile to the regime.

The Rastakhiz party, abandoned by its members and with its government funding discontinued, decided to dissolve itself. Its departure took on a symbolic character and indicated the bankruptcy of the Shah's policy. Gone forever were the sovereign's cherished dreams of the "great civilization" and "the people united behind the Crown."

The Ayatollah of Najaf left Iraq, was turned back at

the Kuwaiti frontier, and headed for Paris, where he arrived on October 3.

For all that, the strikes did not blow over, and they quickly spread to a number of public bodies, including the universities and the hospitals. On October 9 there were clashes in several towns between the police and students demonstrating in favor of the strikers. The work stoppages gradually took on political overtones: at first the workers demanded the release of their arrested comrades, then of all political prisoners.

In an attempt to reduce the level of agitation, on October 16 the Shah announced a partial amnesty for political prisoners, but it came as a drop in the ocean. Clashes between soldiers and demonstrators continued throughout the country on a greater or lesser scale.

In Tehran thousands of inhabitants gathered at the cemetery of Behechté Zahra in memory of the victims of "Black Friday." The ceremony very quickly turned political, and slogans went up against the Shah. With the importance of religious mourning in Shi'ite practice, the big cemetery in the south of the town was very soon transformed into a regular meeting place.

On Sunday, October 22, large-scale demonstrations broke out in Hamadan. For ten hours the crowd took over the streets, and when the police could not disperse them the Army went into action and opened fire, taking a heavy toll of victims. On Monday the twenty-third the troubles spread to Mashhad and Qom. A mosque near Kerman was burned down by unknown hands. Rumor blamed SAVAK agents.

In the meantime the freedom granted to journalists by Sharif-Emami annoyed the military authorities, who tried to impose censorship in order to prevent the press from passing on Khomeini's watchwords. The journalists then went on strike, and after three days of talks they won their way with the Prime Minister. Strikes went on spreading, while sporadic agitation continued all over the country.

Intrigues Against Sharif-Emami

The many contradictions within the ruling class and its members' constant infighting for influence were reflected inside the government. Thus Houshang Nahavandi, who had formed a third wing of the Rastakhiz party, transformed it at the beginning of September into the "Party of the New Society." In a manifesto published on September 5 he asserted that the Iranian people would not tolerate further questioning of the monarchy and the Revolution of the Shah and the People: "Is it conceivable that the peasants, workers and women who have gained social, political and economic rights in the course of the last fifteen years will stand idly by while all their gains are liquidated?" This attitude conveys the thinking of the Shah himself. At the time of my last audience in April 1978 he told me in substance, "I have given the people everything: education, health, a decent standard of living, social and political rights. In many ways the labor legislation I have granted them goes beyond the most liberal systems in the world. The peasants own the land and the workers get twenty percent of business profits and are going to become shareholders with a forty-nine percent interest. In these conditions, what can the Khomeinis and the Sanjabis do against us?" Lost in his grandiose visions of the "great civilization," the Shah took the ideas decreed in his firmans for hard currency.

The "party" created by Nahavandi did not fool anybody. How could people forget that he had been chief of the Empress's secretariat before entering the government? How could they forget his repressive function while head of the University of Tehran? While some ministers supported him within the Cabinet, others hated him. The various conflicting currents undermined the unity of the government, and the military frowned on the continual concessions granted by Sharif-Emami.

Criticism of the latter also affected the Shah. The hardliners advised the monarch to form a government led by Oveissi, the martial-law administrator. The "old establishment" promoted the candidature of Ali Amini, whose incessant refrain to those who would listen was: "I can save the Shah if he will be content to reign and allow me to govern." The refugees from the Rastakhiz party pushed for an amalgam of military men and civilians, with a view to proceeding with liberalization while muzzling the opposition.

At this juncture Ardeshir Zahedi arrived in Tehran, on Tuesday, September 12. He was said to be the bearer of an important message. Some claimed that he had come to advise the monarch to drop his antipathy toward Amini. Others saw him as a possible prime minister. They were mistaken on both counts. The Shah was bent on finding his own solution to the crisis. In any case he knew the limitations of his former son-in-law (proclaiming in private that Ardeshir was a "bird brain"). In fact Zahedi was carrying a message, and through my American contacts I learned its contents: the United States, which had previously been opposed to a trial of strength, was now leaving the sovereign "fully at liberty" to settle his difficulties. The Shah's entourage hoped that this carte blanche would put an end to his state of indecision.

Sharif-Emami, for his part, did not stand idly by amid these intrigues. "It is Parliament which invested me," he reiterated, "and it is Parliament which can deprive me of its confidence." In short, he had no intention of resigning.

But the situation kept deteriorating throughout the month of October, and on the twenty-sixth, the Shah's birthday, in spite of the release of a thousand prisoners and the continuing state of siege, students demonstrated in the university precincts against the monarch and in favor of Khomeini.

The half-measures against corruption cut no ice. The public saw the arrest of a few former ministers merely as the settlement of some old scores. These people had in fact attempted to sabotage the Prime Minister when he was president of the Senate. In any case, as far as the people were concerned the roots of the corruption grew out of the court itself. The fact that one by one the members of the royal family were making their way abroad was not calculated to relieve any suspicions.

My brother informed me that the Shah had decided to exile his family in order to put a stop to its interference in his affairs. "Then why doesn't he proclaim it openly?" I asked. Through not announcing his reasons publicly, his action against the princes and princesses rebounded on the Shah. Public opinion interpreted these departures as expeditious flight, accusing the royal family of removing wealth which they had "stolen" from the nation. The much vaunted announcement of the "code of conduct" imposed by the Shah on his family fell on deaf ears.

It was then that one of my American contacts warned me about Zahedi's intrigues against my brother. When I consulted an Iranian friend he confirmed the information. Zahedi was attempting to persuade the Shah and the military to arrest a number of people, my brother among them, and offer them up as a sop to public resentment. By the terms of the constitution, the ambassador in Washington argued, the Shah bore no responsibility. By using ex-ministers as scapegoats he would save his throne. That kind of infantile reasoning could have sprung only from a boorish mind blinded by personal grudges. Zahedi often said in my presence that he never read books. His grudge against my brother went back to 1971, when he quarreled with him. My brother offered his resignation as prime minister to the Shah, who then decided to dismiss Zahedi from the Cabinet.

Caught up in their revolutionary euphoria, the people paid no attention to these maneuvers. They gave no credit to the government for any concessions granted, but considered them as victories exacted by their own struggle.

The Political Climate at the End of October

After Black Friday in Tehran the opposition was radicalized. Ayatollahs like Shariat-Madari or laymen like

Sanjabi, who would have been satisfied a month before with a constitutional monarchy with or without the abdication of the Shah, found themselves caught up in the revolutionary process. The bloodstained hands of the sovereign and his Prime Minister made compromise out of the question. Their liberalization measures convinced no one. The campaign against corruption seemed phony, because all the big shots had left the country. Repression was still rampant, to judge by the number of arrests. Many members of the opposition went underground. Sanjabi summed up the situation later when he told a journalist, "At the beginning of 1978 it took a lot of courage to attack the Shah; now it takes a lot to defend him."

Yet many members of the opposition were on tenterhooks. They admitted in private that the Shah's departure could happen only by stages. The growing violence disturbed them, because they felt that the Army's intervention against the demonstrators could not have come without the agreement of the Americans, so that the role of the superpowers could not be ignored. Till now the Soviet Union had kept aloof. It was generally agreed that it had made no attempt to take advantage of the situation, being content merely to keep an eye on developments. But would it keep on doing so if it found an Islamic republic led by politically inexperienced clerics installed on its frontier? And what would the United States do? Would it try to foment a coup, as it had in 1953? In the view of many members of the opposition the very success of their revolution had its attendant dangers. One section of the Shi'ite clergy urged moderation. Thus, Ayatollah Shariat-Madari declared, "Our actions must fall within the framework of the constitution . . ."

But the streets stayed under the influence of Khomeini, whose leadership took a firm hold after eight months of disorder. And the old man of Neauphle-le-Château was now demanding nothing less than the downfall of his sworn enemy. Each passing day strengthened his determination and his grip on the masses.

In Tehran, the Shah, his attention clamored for on all sides, dismayed by his belated awakening to reality, and astounded by the "ingratitude" of the peasants and the workers, was subsiding ever deeper into lethargy and uncertainty. Khomeini's star was rising in the sky of Iran, while the monarch's was fading quickly.

At that time some odd rumors circulated in Iran. It was alleged that certain Western elements connected with the CIA and the Israeli secret services had decided to withdraw their support from the Shah. But why would these circles work against what surely still seemed to be the interest of the West? Supposedly they felt that the Shah was finished. A true democracy in Iran would lead to a Marxist takeover of the country, whereas a government based on Islamic fundamentalism would constitute a solid barrier against Communist expansionism. Nobody could provide any grounds for these rumors, but they became quite widespread and did not fail to encourage the forces of the opposition. They also explain, at least in part, Washington's continual expressions of public support for the Shah.

Sensing that the end was surely near, many wealthy Iranians sent their assets to Swiss banks and emigrated abroad to observe events in safety. According to an anecdote then current in Tehran, one day the Empress expressed her surprise to a courtier about the absence of counterdemonstrations on behalf of the Shah. "In

France in 1968 de Gaulle's supporters organized a big march down the Champs-Élysées. Why aren't our people out?" And the courtier replied, "But, Your Majesty, they are all ready to march—down the Champs-Élysées!"

One day toward the end of October a long-faced Ahmad Mirfendereski (who was to become a minister in Bakhtiar's short-lived Cabinet) came into my office. "Have you read the interview with Khomeini?" he asked.

"No. What does he say?"

"Well, his tone has completely altered. Till now his statements have had more to do with metaphysics— he's been keeping purposely vague. Now he has a real program of government. It's the end of the regime."

That same day my American contact informed me that Zahedi had finally convinced the Shah and the Army chiefs to arrest my brother. I got through to Amir Abbas on the telephone and advised him to leave the country. "Never," he told me in a firm voice. "I am not a coward."

Looking back now on my memories of that late October, I realize that the die was cast.

2
THE MOUNTING DANGER

I shall not make the same mistakes as you.

—The Shah to Jacqueline Grapin,
Le Monde, March 7, 1976

The Buildup to the Crisis

The suddenness with which events developed and expanded in 1978 surprised the whole world. How could things have gone so far without anyone's suspecting?

In fact the signs of the crisis had been visible for some time, but nobody paid attention. As in the famous story by Edgar Allan Poe, the letter was in full view, but the searchers lifted the carpets and examined the walls, looking for secret hiding places.

Ever since 1960 there had been a clear prospect of a possible alliance of the left and the right, workers and civil servants, merchants of the bazaar and modern capitalists, peasants and townsmen, clergy and laity.

But harsh repression by the secret police and the resulting atmosphere of widespread fear maintained a surface calm. Hence the image of Iran as a haven of stability in the ferment of the Middle East.

In 1963 the Shah's initiation of a program of revolutionary reforms raised people's hopes for an instant.

The country seemed to have set out in such a reasonable direction that many intellectuals and technocrats joined in the sovereign's drive for modernization. The group of friends to which I myself belonged reckoned that real economic development would necessarily bring democracy. Hence the thing to do was to support the Shah's reforms and give some impetus to both economic progress and political liberalization. We thought the Shah had finally realized that Iran could not be changed by decree alone. He seemed to us to be determined to introduce legality into a field where maintaining public order meant stifling popular aspirations. Sickened by the continuing survival of feudalism, my friends saw agrarian reform as absolutely necessary. What did it matter if it came from the Shah and not from a revolutionary government?

In order to understand our attitude it is worth recalling the situation in Iran before the 1960s. In his doctoral thesis, published just before World War Two, Dr. Sanjabi, president of the National Front, wrote:

> The present agrarian regime and the seigneurial relations of the landowners and peasants, a legacy of medieval feudalism, demand reforms and even total reorganization. . . . The landowner in Persia is not considered by his peasants as a businessman linked to them by contractual ties, but on the contrary as a chief, a master, a lord. . . . It is the villagers who are responsible for personal services to the lord and his family. . . . The Persian landowner considers the village situated on his own estate as his personal property, and the peasants as . . . his subjects. Also, by means of the legitimate right of ownership of the land, he exercises a right of sovereignty and organization over the village. . . . The

landowner is the intermediary between the peasants and the public authority, an intermediary who totally supplants the latter.

I had the chance to observe the lamentable condition of the country and the hardships of the peasants when I returned to Iran after my studies, during the final months of World War Two.

Iran, December 1944

I shall never forget that reintroduction to my homeland after an absence of fifteen years. At the frontier post at Khorramshahr a sickly-looking customs official with wrinkled skin and a cigarette end stuck between his lips would not stop rummaging in my one suitcase. When I lost patience he said, "Come, come, sir—I've got to go by the rules." A ragged porter whispered in my ear, "You've got to give him money." All I had was my fare to Tehran. Eventually the official had to be satisfied with taking the half kilo of oranges which I had bought at Basra, in Iraq, before I crossed the river.

An old rattletrap of a car with a wooden frame shuddered along a potholed road to take me to the railway station at Ahvaz. The ticket-office windows read "Full up" for several days. It was raining outside, and American Army bulldozers were leveling the road surface. As I walked on undecidedly, my clothes got splashed with mud. Tired out by the journey and feeling desperate about my situation, I was on the point of tears. The

GI driver climbed down from the bulldozer and helped me clean myself up. When I told him my story he took me to a lieutenant in charge of military convoys, who got me a passage on the Trans-Iranian.

I slept as best I could, sandwiched between soldiers smelling of beer and tobacco. At dawn the train stopped in Andimeshk, a little station in the mountains. Hundreds of barefooted adults and children in patched clothing stood watching us, shivering with cold. At one end of the open platform the American Army supply services were serving paper-wrapped sandwiches, fruit and coffee. The soldiers ate their breakfast on the spot and threw the leftovers into drums spaced out along the platform, before reembarking. At once the tattered Iranians rushed to these dustbins and delved into them for the discarded bits of bread, orange peel and banana skins, which they wolfed down greedily.

All over Tehran there was poverty and disease. I was staying with cousins, and we slept four to every small room. In the streets beggars dogged our footsteps in gangs of ten or more. The Allies frequented clubs displaying signs "Iranians and dogs forbidden."

In the spring of 1945, friends took me to their estate in the Mazandaran region, near Sari, to celebrate the Iranian New Year. The peasants moldered in their huts and ate two meals consisting of a crust of bread and some yoghurt, because the landowner kept nearly all the rice crop for himself. I felt as if I had been carried backward in time. The bailiff kept the workers under strict supervision and punished them if they tried to avoid their statutory labor obligations.

In the capital, Parliament, despite Iran's "free" elections, was still in the hands of the big landowners and the upper bourgeoisie. The situation looked desperate. Most of my friends stayed for a short while and then left again for the West, now that the war was over and communications were restored.

The country was stagnating in misery, and there seemed to be no end in view. It was in these conditions that the reforms announced by the Shah and submitted to a national referendum kindled a gleam of hope in some eyes. It would be unjust to ignore the spectacular achievements which took place after 1965 and to judge the regime only on the last two years of the reign of the Pahlavis. In fact, until 1972 the country was making significant progress.

The Credit Side

Once the 1963 riots had been quelled, things seemed to go better. Despite the persistence of authoritarianism, there were real economic and social gains.

Domestically, agrarian reform caused the political influence of the feudal landowners and the aristocracy to break down for the first time in centuries. The dismissal of the founder of SAVAK, the sadistic General Teymur Bakhtiar, cousin of Shahpur Bakhtiar, and his replacement by Hassan Pakravan, a more humane type of soldier, cleared the air a little. Calling in a team of young men under the leadership of Hassan Ali Mansour to take over from the professional politicians opened up new perspectives for the rising generations.

In the sphere of foreign policy the Shah rather kept his distance from the West and turned slightly toward his powerful neighbor in the north, concluding commercial and cultural agreements with Moscow. What he called his "policy of national independence" was beginning to take shape. He pledged himself not to allow any foreign military bases on Iranian soil.

In their speeches both the Soviet leaders and the Shah of Iran cited their neighborly relations as a good example. I felt that the Shah was sincere in this new line. I well remember his euphoria after the signing of the Russo-Iranian agreement for the construction of the new steelworks at Esfahan. That was in 1966. He gave me a friendly welcome in the palace built by his father right in the center of the capital. "That's it!" he cried triumphantly. "We've just signed the contract with the Russians. The steelworks that the Westerners refused us will soon be standing on the banks of the Zayinda Rud. Heavy industry will guarantee our independence!"

The news was greeted with general enthusiasm. Ever since prewar days the steelworks had become a special symbol because it had been resisted by the British, who then dominated the country. The writer Sadeq Tchubak later told me a story of how he had been visiting the bazaar and had asked one of the merchants, "Haji Agha, don't you want to go to Mecca to ease your bones?" "Of course I do," came the answer, "but I'm waiting for the steelworks. With that, everything will go better."

And that was how things were looking in that spring of 1966. There was no more talk of the December 1964 assassination of Prime Minister Mansour. (A group of religious fanatics was accused at the time. Some people saw in it a plot hatched by foreign powers.) The attempt on the Shah's life in March 1965 also seemed ancient history. Nobody yet saw any special significance in Pakravan's replacement as head of SAVAK by General Nasiri. My brother's appointment as prime minister put a temporary brake on the maneuverings of the various political factions. The country was like one vast building site. The growth rate fluctuated between nine and twelve percent, per-capita income was rising slowly but surely, and at one meeting of the Central Treaty Organization (CENTO—the military pact of Iran, Pakistan, Turkey and Britain, with American participation) the Shah confidentially informed American Secretary of State Dean Rusk, "You see, all is going well. My Prime Minister is a man of modest origins, and his brother, a left-wing intellectual, has decided to take his place in the service of the nation."

And in 1977, when the Shah dismissed my brother as prime minister after a little over a dozen years of service, the country presented a different face. More than sixty-five percent of the population owned the houses they lived in (and the percentage was even higher in the capital). Per-capita income stood at $2,200 ($300 in 1965). Primary-school attendance was over ten million (270,000 in 1960). Illiteracy had fallen from eighty-five to fifty-five percent. Whereas oil revenues had accounted for ninety percent of the gross national product in the 1950s, in 1977 they came to no more than thirty-five percent (for a total of $70 billion). The present critics of the regime claim that industry was confined to assembly. They forget that in the car industry, for example, in 1977 more than sixty-five percent of components were manufactured in Iran. Agriculture, although it left a lot to be desired, was showing real and appreciable progress, as the events of 1978–79 have proved. (In fact, although almost all Iran's foodstuff imports were paralyzed, there was never any shortage of food supplies either in Tehran or in any of the other towns. And it is worth mentioning that from 1972 to 1977 domestic consumption had quadrupled.) In the fields of communications, social welfare, health, education, etc., the picture was equally impressive. If inflation, which had remained reasonable until 1975, began galloping in 1977, it is generally agreed that this was the outcome of the sudden injection of Iran's increased revenues from oil.

I have felt it necessary to recall these facts because a balanced verdict on the regime ought not to lose sight of the achievements of the previous fifteen years. In fact, the Shah's basic fault at that stage of the country's development was not so much to do with accelerated economic development as with the neglect of political liberties. By 1970–72 the improvement in material conditions was requiring a parallel move toward democratization. Here the sovereign committed a serious error of judgment and let slip a number of opportunities. Yet as early as 1971 the appearance of guerrilla activity, even on a small scale, ought to have alerted him.

Siahkal, Mazandaran, April 10, 1971

A group of guerrillas unknown to the Shah's secret police made a surprise attack on the police station near the village of Siahkal, in the Mazandaran Mountains overlooking the Caspian. Far from showing any concern about this incident, the authorities stressed the cooperation of the peasants recently turned landowners in the arrest of the seven "terrorists." An isolated act with no likely repercussions, so the SAVAK experts decided.

But the guerrillas changed their tactics, abandoning the rural areas hostile to their slogans, to concentrate their efforts in the big towns. In the autumn of 1971 they assassinated General Farsian, prosecutor of the Tehran military tribunal, and attack followed attack as the years went on. SAVAK once again became the ruthless instrument of repression which it had been at the start. Instead of encouraging liberalism, as he had implied that he would, the Shah fortified his authority and transformed himself from enlightened monarch into ruthless tyrant.

The relative liberalism of 1965 was succeeded by a suffocating authoritarianism. Late in 1970 my brother returned from his weekly audience and told me, "I don't know what's happening to him. He doesn't listen anymore. Discussions get on his nerves."

What had happened? Was it the prospect of filling the "vacuum" left in the Persian Gulf by the departure of the British that stoked the Shah's ambitions? Was it the installation of his friend Nixon in the White House that fired his imagination? Was it the proximity of his former son-in-law Zahedi that made him take a turn to the right? Had some blood vessel burst in his brain?

With hindsight it is possible to put a date on the shifting perspective of the Shah's vision. It seems to go back to Nixon's being returned for a second term as President of the United States, and to the rapid rise of a newcomer in the firmament of American diplomacy: Henry Kissinger.

Tehran, Tuesday, May 30, 1972: The Nixon Visit

Leaving Moscow, where he had just signed important agreements with Leonid Brezhnev, and before going on to Warsaw, President Nixon made a long detour to visit Tehran. This tiring side trip seemed all the more incomprehensible because he had already had discussions with the Shah the previous year, when he stopped at Tehran on his way to Peking.

Nixon intended to kill two birds with one stone. First he would make amends for the insult to the Shah of sending Vice-President Agnew to represent the President at the 2500th anniversary celebrations, and then he would underline the new importance of Iran for the United States. Henceforth the Shah was no longer a vassal but a peer.

Over the previous three years, secret tripartite negotiations among Iran, the United States and the United Kingdom had produced a solution to the problem of the "vacuum" left by the British in the Gulf. The Shah agreed to the proclamation of independence by Bahrein in return for Iranian occupation of a number of strategic islands defending the Strait of Hormuz (the two Tunbs and half of Abu Musa). Nixon found this arrangement an excellent trial run for his "doctrine" according to which the friends of the United States ought to assume responsibility for their own defense. Iran could provide the Gulf emirates with the same protection that the Americans gave in other regions. And the Shah offered to foot the bill himself—an extra bonus. Kissinger had come with the President, and he was exultant: his "grand design" of an axis reaching from Australia to South Africa by way of the Middle Eastern oil fields was beginning to take shape. By the secret agreement concluded in Tehran, the Shah received carte blanche in his purchase of weapons.

This was a real turning point in American policy, because hitherto it had been the U.S. which determined the nature and quantity of armaments and advised the monarch about the policy to follow. In Lyndon Johnson's time the Shah had shown his annoyance by turning toward the USSR and Britain. In any case his relations with Democratic Presidents were never good. In private he lost no opportunity to criticize Roosevelt, Johnson and especially John F. Kennedy. "The Democrats are playing into the Russians' hands," he once told one of his ministers, in my presence. "It is not surprising that the Communists are taking advantage of them to extend their empire."

Instead of moderating the Shah and easing him along the way to democratization, Nixon and Kissinger encouraged his authoritarianism. One witness to the Tehran meeting told me that Nixon said to the Shah, "I envy the way you deal with your students. . . . Pay no attention to our liberals' griping."

A hug from Nixon as he left Tehran sealed the Shah's new status as "defender of the West."

It is safe to say that most of the subsequent difficulties of the regime date from that day. In fact, these developments aroused the distrust of every country in the region, and particularly of the Soviet Union. (The radio station Peyké Iran resumed its hostile transmissions from somewhere in Eastern Europe.) As for the Shah, intoxicated by his new position, he launched into an ambitious arms program which was to destroy the economic and political balance of the country. He even forgot the basic weakness of his regime, based on the rule of a single man governing by decree; the absence of any transition mechanism was to make itself grievously felt in the last days of December 1978.

The secret agreement with Nixon and Kissinger on the protection of the Gulf and the Indian Ocean deflected the Shah from his original course. Eager to taste the fruits of his new power right away, he did not even wait for them to ripen, but picked them green. He went too far, and became his own worst enemy. It was two events of his own causing which were to backfire and bring about his downfall: namely, the rise in the price of oil in 1973–74 and the change of direction in domestic policy in 1977.

Niavaran Palace, Tehran, December 1973: The Oil Boom

The Shah rubbed his hands with delight as he waited to address the foreign journalists for his extraordinary press conference. He had just quadrupled his country's income and made a resounding entry upon the international scene. And the nation would be eternally grateful. After all, Mossadeq had only nominally nationalized Iran's black gold, whereas he, Mohammad Reza Pahlavi, had poured fabulous sums into his country's treasury. With those extra billions he would increase the tempo of development. In his own lifetime Iran was going to be "the fifth industrial and military power" in the world. He would be the equal of the supremos of this world, he, the great politician who had just brought to their knees the Seven Sisters, those oil companies which had been considered more powerful than the superpowers.

A few days afterward, he presided over a restricted economic council. My brother and two ministers, Hushang Ansari and Majid Majidi, tried in vain to prevent him from injecting that entire surplus into the economy at one stroke. They suggested using fifty percent immediately, and the rest gradually, year by year. The Shah turned a deaf ear; he ordered the revision of the fifth five-year plan, which had been operating for only a year. Furthermore, he changed the economic priorities in favor of heavy industry and the Army.

(My brother told me how on several occasions, both in and out of the Supreme Economic Council, he pressed the Shah to reduce military expenditure in favor of the social sector, stop purely prestige projects, turn down contracts cooked up inside court circles, and reasonably balance the economy. But at that time, under the impact of the sudden growth of the nation's resources, the Shah believed more than ever in the automatic virtue of capital accumulation and increased spending. He suffered from the naïve belief that money can do anything, ignoring the rules of finance and taking no account of the consequences of a sudden jump in spending. Inflation was inevitable when in the space of a few years the budget mounted from two to fifty billion dollars.)

After 1976 we witnessed a regular gold rush. All the world's businessmen flocked to Tehran like bees around a honeypot. As for the Iranians, they queued up around the court and its hangers-on for their own share of the cake. Middlemen proliferated, extorting huge sums solely for putting foreigners in touch with the higher officials in charge of executing the Shah's ambitious programs. Various European ex-royals secured some stupendous contracts for European manufacturers thanks to their entree at court. Prosperity came on the scene, with its retinue of injustice and corruption.

Western governments and business circles, confronted with unprecedented economic difficulties, blamed the Shah for his crucial role in the decision of the Organization of Petroleum Exporting Countries (OPEC) to raise the price of oil.

A week after the price rise, John Scali, the American ambassador to the United Nations, buttonholed me in a corridor of the UN to ask, "Why have you pulled this trick? It's hard to swallow, coming from a friend." In March 1974, as I was going into the Côte Basque restaurant, I saw shipping magnate Aristotle Onassis sitting talking to five people. I overheard one sentence starting "As for the Shah, there's only one—" He broke off when he saw me, waved a greeting, and went on: "We'll discuss it later." Was he planning a counterattack?

Whether or not it was staged by Onassis and his friends, that counterattack came in a curious form. The Western nations took draconian steps to "save" oil. Exports of black gold did not rise, contrary to the Shah's optimistic forecasts, and at the same time his grandiose projects and arms purchases rapidly absorbed the increase in oil revenues. Refusing to modify his demands, the sovereign attempted to sell more oil, but the customers were anything but enthusiastic. The five-year plan had to be revised all over again.

Yet, despite the difficulties, my brother's government managed to establish a reserve of twelve billion dollars. To this must be added the loans made to the International Bank and a number of individual countries (the new regime has been taking advantage of the repayment of these same loans to keep the country going).

Be that as it may, despite my brother's insistence, the sovereign refused to cut military spending and ordered economies in the social sector. Not that he was losing his illusions. In the summer of 1975, as I was talking to him about the need for Iran to stay inside the ranks of the Third World nations, the Shah broke in curtly to say, "We are not an undeveloped country anymore!" He was already considering a further boost in the price of oil to make up for the shortfall in earnings resulting from the drop in exports.

But late in 1976 financial difficulties forced him to change his tune. Until then he had been fond of the slogan "Get rich!" In October 1976, in an interview arranged at his own prompting with the newspaper *Kayhan*, he broadly explained that the people must put in greater efforts in order to "merit" their new status:

"[Till now] we have not asked the people for sacrifices. Instead we have kept them wrapped in cotton wool. Things are going to change now. Everyone will have to work harder and be ready for sacrifices in the national interest. The party has been given the task of inculcating this new state of mind."* Obviously a program like this was not calculated to make the regime more popular.

Now Shahr, Iran, August 5, 1977

The Shah, in shirt sleeves, received my brother in the wooden cabin, built on piles, which he used as a drawing room. He informed him point-blank that he meant to replace him with Amuzegar, and offered him the job of minister of the court, where he said that there was much to be done, in both the domestic and the external field. Amir Abbas was not deceived; he knew that the sovereign had just given him the sack. Certainly the Court Ministry was a position of trust, but that was another matter. At that point the Empress came in, and the Shah told her what he intended.

"Hoveyda is one of us," he said. "He'll be able to arrange the Court Ministry as we wish."

Farah smiled. "Yes, provided you give him a broom to sweep the nest clean of all the corrupt people who are occupying it!"

* *Kayhan International,* October 30, 1976.

Amir Abbas felt relieved. Early that year he had told one of his friends who paid him an early-morning visit, "Every night when I go to bed I pray to the Almighty to recall me to Him during my sleep. I've had enough. The Shah has overloaded the ship of state. He wants me to take it in tow, but I can't, it's too heavy."

Psychologically speaking, Amuzegar was the opposite of my brother. He was an excitable, bad-tempered man, on distant terms with colleagues and public alike. He made no attempt to handle them with tact like Amir Abbas, who always tried to smooth things out so as to keep the balance among the various forces acting in the country. For Amuzegar economics came before politics. He surrounded himself with young technocrats, to the exclusion of experienced politicians.

From that moment onward, serious mistakes were committed. Given the nature of the regime, obviously the blame cannot be laid upon Amuzegar. In fact, the Shah had decided on a change of course. He felt that my brother had been too soft with the opposition. (Amir Abbas was in touch with various members of the opposition through the medium of personal friends like Gholam Mossadeq, the son of the former Prime Minister, and another man linked with religious circles, whose name I cannot reveal here for obvious reasons. With a bare handful of other ministers, he even advised the sovereign to open a dialogue with his opponents. Besides that, his "obsession" with fighting high-level corruption irritated the Shah, who told him a month before the change of government, "Honesty is not enough.") He considered it necessary to take a harder line. Amuzegar's words at the meeting of the party political bureau on the occasion of the demonstrations of January 9, 1979 (which I reported in Part One), reflected the will of the sovereign. In the economic sphere too, his impatience drove him to order exorbitant measures. For instance, he wanted to bring inflation down to zero.

Consequently Amuzegar put a squeeze on credit and made spectacular cuts in public spending (except, of course, for armaments, the Shah's private domain). The small manufacturers and tradesmen, particularly the shopkeepers of the bazaar, were grievously affected by the stopping of low-interest loans. Legislation for the compulsory reduction of rents made no alteration whatsoever to the position of rich people who owned a lot of real estate: they simply stopped letting their property, because they could afford to live on capital. But the middle classes were caught in a vice. Often they owned two apartments and were living in one and using the rent from the other to finance their children's studies abroad. All at once they found themselves compelled to borrow money on the black market at prohibitive rates. The fight against land speculation raged so fiercely that it put a stop to all transactions, and the building industry suffered as a result.

In his relentless drive to cut spending, Amuzegar abruptly canceled the funding that my brother had made available for religious purposes, amounting to about eleven million dollars a year. This money, charged against the secret budget of the Prime Minister, was used to finance the upkeep of the country's mosques and Koranic schools, as well as for various other expenses. In this way my brother was attempting to make up for losses suffered by the clergy as a result of agrarian reform, which had affected some of the lands traditionally administered by them. These grants were for the benefit of all the clergy, including the supporters of Khomeini.

And if that was not enough, Amuzegar announced the inauguration of a plan to reduce the heavy traffic in Tehran. It involved extending the north–south expressway to pass through the site of the Tehran bazaar. Immediately the bazaar was pervaded by rumors that the Shah wanted to destroy their tradespeople's shops and disperse them.

After the Amuzegar government's drastic cuts and the announcement of this plan, discontent spread among religious circles, the middle classes, and the tradesmen in the bazaars as well.

The new Prime Minister also offended the regime's supporters with his often cavalier manners. There were times when he acted on government decisions before having them ratified by Parliament. Once, when challenged by the deputy Bani-Ahmad on the subject of the riots in Tabriz, he got his Minister of Justice to stand in for him. Many deputies felt insulted. Inside the Rastakhiz party, where he had assumed control, he also quarreled with the leadership' of the three wings, feeling that they were spending their time stirring up rank-and-file criticism against the government.

Just a few months after the inauguration of the new government, demonstrations broke out and grew in scale. The Army and the police fired into the crowds and caused many casualties.*

Nobody had understood the reasons for the change

---

* I must point out here that the list of "expendables" issued by the present Islamic Tribunal mentions all former Prime Ministers except for Amuzegar and Amini.

of government in any case. If the Shah wanted to pla-
cate the growing political opposition he should have
called in a more popular figure. Furthermore, Amuzegar had held important posts in every Cabinet, including my brother's, for sixteen years running, so if there
was blame to be laid he shared in it. And when he
made speeches or was quoted in the press as criticizing
the actions of the previous government, he could not
generate any credibility.

. The "new" policy inaugurated by the Shah failed to
pay off in any sphere. In about a year the economy was
heading for a stoppage of business, investment had
slumped disastrously, and social problems were worsening.*

The Roots of the Crisis

If the three events mentioned above—the Nixon visit
to Tehran in 1972, the oil boom, and the change of
course in 1977—explain the acceleration of the crisis,
its taproot lay in the dictatorial character of the regime
itself. The Shah took most of the decisions on his own,

* At the time of his mock trial, Amir Abbas asked his masked so-called
judges, "Have you asked yourselves why the Shah fired me from the post of
prime minister in 1977, then from the post of minister of the court in 1978?"
He would have gone on to explain why, but he was not allowed the time.
The reason for those successive dismissals lay in his growing disagreement
with the sovereign over several points, in particular the campaign against
corruption at the top, in the monarch's family and entourage, and dialogue
with the opposition. He told me himself that it was his opposition to the
Shah's orders to open fire on demonstrators early in September 1978 which
had caused his "resignation" from the post of minister of the court.

and did his utmost to discourage criticism, even among his closest advisers. In the circumstances, rather than expose themselves to his wrath, his ministers preferred to submit even the most trivial problems to him in advance. I will quote a single instance out of many. The Minister of Health told me in 1977 that, concerned about the increasing number of stray dogs, he had presented a report to the sovereign, and received permission to get rid of them. But as he was preparing to issue the necessary instructions the Shah sent for him and told him, "Don't do anything for now. My sister is an animal lover; she has got wind of it and she's giving me a hard time. But she leaves for Europe next month, and you can go ahead then." He considered it quite normal that he should be consulted even on the most minor details.

His conception of the monarchy harked back to the distant past. Concerning this question, he once wrote: "The special character of the Iranian monarchy implies, as Christensen says, that a true king of this country is not solely the Head of State but at the same time the guide and teacher of the people."* This concept was so deep-rooted in his mind that he did not hesitate to declare in one interview, "Basically the King, in our country, is the chief of all three powers—executive, legislative and judiciary."† In other words, three centuries after Louis XIV he was proclaiming, "L'État, c'est moi."

One day I heard him tell his entourage, "I hire officials, and I fire them." I had a chance to verify that the hard way when, following my brother's arrest in 1978,

* *Towards the Great Civilization.*
† Olivier Warin, *Le Lion et le soleil.*

I considered leaving my job. A SAVAK agent (someone I knew, though I didn't know whom he worked for) called me and said, "You're talking too much. Be careful. Your brother is in jail. And then think of your family, and your children."

The Governments in the Government

There was no single government in Iran under the Shah, but several centers of influence under his aegis, with their ministers in direct contact with him.

Thus, Amir Asadullah Alam, who was minister of the court until August 1977, took decisions affecting the national economy with the agreement of the Shah, and executed them on his own. It was the same with Dr. Eqbal, the manager of the National Iranian Oil Company. The Army also enjoyed a broad degree of independence. As for SAVAK, it was only nominally attached to the office of the Prime Minister.

Under these conditions it became impossible to coordinate the various activities of the country. The whole system was undermined by a kind of feudal fragmentation. My brother tried to sail these treacherous waters by relying on a handful of close collaborators, but the Shah became more and more authoritarian, going his own way regardless of advice. Although he would still listen to my brother's complaints (but paid them no heed), he reacted very heatedly to other people's criticism. That was what caused him to fire his chief of staff, General Djam, in 1971 when the General was critical of the Shah's tactical plans in the conflict with Iraq.

The Shah's Initiatives

The sovereign often dredged up his ideas at random from his conversations with foreign visitors. For instance, an Iranian American once mentioned "agribusiness" to him, and he at once decided that this formula would enable Iran to boost its level of output at one stroke and become an exporter of foodstuffs. He immediately gave orders for "agribusiness" to be introduced around the big dams in the south. Peasants who had only just received their title deeds found themselves compelled to exchange them for nominal shares and then to enroll as wage earners in the new intensive farming enterprises. Of course they were profoundly disillusioned. For people who had barely emerged from the medieval night of feudalism, land was a palpable good, and "shares" were just paper. On top of that they had a feeling of going back to square one when they found themselves working for some faceless business which took the place of the big landowners dislodged by Iran's agrarian reforms. The same frustration developed among the peasants pitchforked into government cooperatives. Unable to express their grievances freely, they voted with their feet against the alien intruder "modernization" by leaving the villages to look for work in the towns. The Shah's programs very soon ran into trouble, and agricultural output did not make the strides he expected.

In the industrial sector too, the Shah's impatience and visions of grandeur produced difficulties. Heavy industry, petrochemistry and atomic power stations required expertise which could not be found in the country. The Shah reacted to this situation by bringing in far too many foreign technicians.

During the final months of the regime it was often alleged that the speed of the modernization program had cost the Shah his throne. The truth is that his basic mistake was his manner of putting it into practice.

Corruption

Every Iranian government for fifty years has written the struggle against corruption into its program, but corruption expanded beyond all acceptable bounds after the oil boom of 1974. I remember a visit to my brother in August 1976 when I asked him why the country's businessmen and industrialists made no donations to culture and the arts. There was anger in his voice as he replied, "We don't need their money. The biggest service they could render would be to stop stealing!" I then asked the inevitable question: "Why don't you take them to court?" He gave me a despondent look. "I don't take them to court? I do nothing else but take them to court! But what's the use? The campaign has to begin at the top, with the Shah's family and entourage.

Otherwise it's pointless. And anyway it isn't fair to hit the minnows when the big fish are getting away."

Corruption ran wild at the heart of the royal family. The Shah's brothers and sisters earned exorbitant commissions on contracts by acting as go-betweens, usually through companies in which they were the majority shareholders. I shall return to this question later. For the moment it suffices to say that the example of the royal family was a source of contamination which infected every level of society. Colossal fortunes were made in the time it takes to sign a contract. The scandals multiplied remorselessly. A Senate inquiry in the United States revealed that many people, including the Shah's brother-in-law, the Air Force chief, and Princess Ashraf's eldest son, had collected sizable bribes. It came out later that Admiral Ramzi Attai, commander in chief of the Navy, had pocketed more than three million dollars on military contracts.

One of the deputy ministers of health told me in 1977 that the Shah's personal doctor, a high-ranking Army officer who had no responsibility in government, had been foisted on him to supervise the importation and local production of all medicinal supplies. On the Shah's orders the Ministry of Health had set up a bank for the construction of hospitals throughout the country, but members of the royal family exerted their influence in the distribution of contracts.

Again in 1977 the sovereign launched a program of free meals for schoolchildren, under the supervision of the Empress's mother. A friend told me that in one Caspian town the truck drivers responsible for delivering food to one particular school resold it on the open market for profit.

Faced with the rapid growth of corruption, in the

spring of 1976 the Shah decided to take stern measures against it. A number of big merchants and industrialists ran into trouble, but despite a few spectacular sentences the public remained skeptical. That was because as early as 1971 (after the attempt on the life of the King of Morocco) the Shah had agreed to my brother's request to deal severely with his own family. He even exiled one of his nephews for a while. But a few months later the nephew was back at his old tricks.

My brother set up a special commission of inquiry to investigate under-the-counter payments made by foreign companies to people in high places. Since one of the top officials of one of these companies happened to be in Tehran at the time, he was called to appear, and was forbidden to leave the country. But the person in question did not turn up before the commission. My brother learned subsequently that he had been driven to a departing plane in a court vehicle (members of the royal family did not have to go through customs and police formalities). As for the Iranian VIPs implicated in these matters, they took long vacations in Europe.

Fact and fantasy merged. Everybody fed names into the rumor mill, either for amusement or through malice, and the names then became public property.

The fight against corruption was not an easy one in these conditions. The correspondent of Le Monde went so far as to describe it as "a near-impossible task, bearing in mind that the Emperor himself is not above all reproach in this sphere."* According to one American expert the Pahlavi Foundation created by the sovereign had become an open method of enriching the royal

* Le Monde, October 3, 1978.

family.* And since the princes and certain exalted figures remained invulnerable, the public had little belief
in the Shah's sincerity. In any case the sovereign enter-
tained some quite bizarre opinions on this subject. I
have already quoted what he told my brother. In reply
to Olivier Warin's remark "It is said that corruption
does not preclude some members of your own entourage," the Shah declared, "All things are possible, but
in this particular case it would not be corruption, it
would simply be behaving like all the rest, in other
words like people who have every right to work and do
business, and who in the same circumstances would be
considered to be legally quite entitled to work for a
living."†

Repression

I have said already that SAVAK was only nominally
attached to the government. In practice it acted inde-
pendently and took its orders from the Shah himself.
Its activities were carried on in the utmost secrecy. It
did its best to foster an atmosphere of fear which poi-
soned the country's society from top to bottom. No one
dared speak openly. When my friends wanted to tell
me a secret they took me out into the garden and low-
ered their voices. Now and then I learned of the arrest
of members of the opposition, and then I would use my

* *Armed Forces Journal,* January 1979.
† Olivier Warin, *Le Lion et le soleil.*

brother's good offices to intervene with the Shah and try to save lives. Informers were a dime a dozen.

When the campaign conducted by Amnesty International and other international organizations revealed the scale of arbitrary arrest and torture in Iran, I was able, through my brother, to arrange a visit by their representatives. That was why delegates from Amnesty, the Red Cross, the International Commission of Jurists, etc., were able to visit the prisons. Their reports led to the cessation of torture and a reduction of arbitrary practices.

Censorship was heavy-handed, and it was not uncommon for SAVAK to confiscate books which had previously been authorized. Performances of *Hamlet* or *Macbeth* were forbidden for the simple reason that a king or a prince was murdered in them. Films were cut at will. One friend of mine, Ebrahim Golestan, had a film banned because his fable about a nouveau riche might elicit comparisons with the story of the Shah after the oil boom. One writer spent several nights in a SAVAK jail solely because one of the regime's opponents quoted a sentence from one of his books in an intercepted letter.

Torture was eventually banned by the Shah, but it was a subject that drew some quite cynical remarks from him on occasion. In an interview televised in the United States on October 24, 1976, Mike Wallace asked him, "If torture proves necessary, do you use it?" The sovereign answered, "Not torture in the old sense, in the sense of twisting arms and doing this and that. But nowadays there are intelligent means of questioning people."

Executions were usually announced only after the

event. The Shah did not consider guerrillas as "politicals" but simply as "terrorists." As for drug smugglers, there was a special law authorizing their instant execution. The families thus plunged into mourning harbored bitter grudges against the monarch. Late in 1976 a visiting colleague from the Foreign Ministry told me in New York, "The Shah's heart is getting harder and harder."

Drugs

Iranians were particularly contemptuous about the Shah's crackdown on drugs. One of the Shah's brothers, Mahmoud Reza, had been given permission to cultivate the poppy and to sell opium. (In fact, according to the Tehran grapevine, every year he claimed that the harvest had been a poor one, and kept back large amounts of opium, which he sold at high prices on the black market.) They also recalled the notorious scandal in Switzerland in 1972 when one of the members of the Shah's retinue, Amir Hushang Davalou, with a warrant out against him for drug dealing, got away from the local forces of justice. The Shah himself drove him to a plane waiting at the Zurich airport, under the eyes of the helpless police. The affair caused a lot of commotion in the Swiss and European press at the time. The censors kept the news out of the country, but word of mouth followed its inexorable course, and the man in the street wondered how it came about that a few petty smugglers were shot down on the Shah's instructions, while the same Shah was prepared to rescue his friend from the prisons of Switzerland. I remember how that spring my brother protested to the Shah and offered his resignation, and withdrew to his house on the Caspian for several days. But the Shah rejected his resignation. As for Amir Hushang Davalou, he dropped out of sight for a few months and then turned up again at court as casual as you please.

As well as that, there were "smokers" in the entourage of the princes and princesses. Now and then the Shah would fly off the handle about this, whereupon the culprits would creep off to indulge their pleasures elsewhere, returning when the imperial wrath had abated.

Immorality

Certain members of the royal family and high society openly led lives of which the very least that can be said is that they respected neither the commandments of the state religion nor even the most basic morality.

At the prompting of his Minister of the Court, Alam, and Alam's hangers-on, the Shah even authorized the establishment of casinos and "pleasure resorts" in Iran. The stated motive was to attract the Gulf sheikhs, for reasons both political and economic. Gambling establishments sprang up in several towns, sometimes with the participation of members of the royal family. The island of Kish in the Persian Gulf became a vacation center for billionaires, at great expense, and not without a heavy drain in misappropriated funds. (Rumor had it that Air France's Concorde flights were used to import women chosen by the famous Madame Claude of Paris.) The deal was launched on the pretext of "encouraging tourism," but when it exceeded its target costs and did not fulfill its promoters' hopes, there was an unsuccessful attempt made to force the National Iranian Oil Company and the Iran National Airlines Corporation to buy up the real estate on Kish. An acquaintance of mine, present at one of the meetings concerning the sale of these installations, told me that the head of Iran Air asked to examine the profitability of the venture, which earned him a sarcastic retort from the sovereign.

The reader need only recall the Islamic prohibition on alcohol and gambling to understand the damaging effect of these activities on the masses. Besides that, there were rumors in Tehran about Princess Ashraf's gambling losses in foreign casinos. Word also had it that Princess Shams had become a convert to the Roman Catholic faith.

The capital was split into two separate towns: to the north, a wealthy metropolis, living in European-style luxury villas surrounded by restaurants, discotheques and nightclubs; to the south a poverty-stricken city of narrow alleys and polluted air, inhabited by the poor.

The influx of foreign civilian and military technicians which went with importing sophisticated technologies enhanced the "Westernization" of life in the big towns. Western influence extended through every sphere. Millions of dollars were spent on drawing up the plans for a modern city in the center of Tehran, the "Shahestan Pahlavi," which was to contain skyscrapers going up to sixty stories. (The project was abandoned, having suffered considerably from embezzlement.) Imitation of

the Americans even found its way into the Shah's
methods of government: in 1978, when he dismissed
Nasiri from his office as head of SAVAK, he sent him
as ambassador to Pakistan, just as Nixon had appointed Richard Helms, the former director of the CIA,
as his ambassador to Tehran.

The Enormous Arsenal

In a period of twenty-one years, from 1950 to 1971,
purchases of arms from the United States did not
exceed a billion dollars. Between 1971 and 1978 they
reached the astronomical figure of nineteen billion.*

Such a situation could not leave the Soviet Union
unmoved, especially when the Shah gave the Americans permission to install an electronic surveillance
network near the northern frontier, capable of detect-
ing the launching of missiles.

In 1976 my brother broke his journey in Moscow on
his way back from a visit to Mongolia, and had a meeting with Premier Alexei Kosygin. The Soviet Prime
Minister bitterly attacked Iran's purchases of arms. Before then, right after the Nixon visit in 1972, the Shah
had made a private visit to the USSR at the invitation of Brezhnev. One of the officials who accompanied
him told me that in the course of a secret meeting

---

* In 1978, sixty-five percent of all expenditure went for defense, steelworks, atomic power and the petrochemical industry.

the Russians had asked him to stop the arms race. The Shah refused, and the talks were completely deadlocked.

In September of the same year, when our Foreign Minister met Andrei Gromyko in New York, the Russian told him, with a trace of humor, "All these arms you're equipping yourselves with are making us think—"

Our Minister cut in: "It's a matter of the defense of Iran. Our policy is not directed against our great neighbor to the north. Whatever we do, we can never equal your power."

"Certainly," Gromyko went on. "But we wonder why, and against whom. Iraq? But that is a small country. The Emirates? They don't count militarily. Saudi Arabia? It is no threat to Iran. Then why?"

Our Minister had no valid argument available, and he changed the subject.

The following year, during a session of the General Assembly, a high-ranking Soviet diplomat said to me, "Until these recent years you have practiced a policy of balance which has favored the development of our relations. We know that you have a position of privilege with the United States, and we accept that. But with your appetite for advanced weaponry you are on your way to upsetting the balance."

Irrespective of the balance of power, the bottomless pit of military spending was certainly swallowing the greater part of Iran's oil revenues. Ill-considered arms purchases were putting the entire economy in danger. The evidence of the reports of the Supreme Economic Council chaired by the Shah himself shows that my brother and a few of his ministers tried to moderate the sovereign's appetites, but he remained obsessed by his dream of transforming Iran into a military power.*

In the summer of 1977 I was discussing this problem with my brother. "Don't get the idea that a Prime Minister knows all and sees all in Iran," he told me. "There are any number of fields which the Shah keeps completely to himself. Like SAVAK, and the Army. He informs us about military contracts after the event, and compels us to make cuts in other plans. Take our intervention in Oman, for instance: I learned about that only with the announcement of battles in which our own troops were engaged." And when I remained silent he added, "Listen, I personally have nothing to blame myself for. I haven't got rich in my job. I have never given criminal orders. My hands are not bloodstained. And I believe that I have served my country, in spite of the very difficult conditions I work under."

The Deterioration of the Economy

With the mounting prosperity, Iranians started looking to the outside world in increasing numbers. Not only

---

* In a June 1979 interview in *Penthouse*, Paul Erdman, author of *The Crash of '79*, rejecting the theories which attribute the fall of the Shah to the speed of his modernization program, says in substance: If the monarch had not frittered away the country's resources on military spending, if he had contented himself with taking a billion dollars for himself and another billion for his generals, and had concentrated the rest on development, his son would have succeeded him on the throne. Without going as far as Erdman, it can be said that military spending was one of the main causes of the country's economic problems, and consequently of the rapid downfall of the regime.

the rich but the middle classes too started buying property in Europe and the United States. Visiting Nice in 1976, I was struck by the growing number of Iranians. I even suggested that they should change the name of the Promenade des Anglais to Promenade des Iraniens. The Shah kept turning a deaf ear to my brother and his economic experts when they urged him to take steps to restrict the export of capital. What he said to my brother was along the lines of "They've earned the money, they're entitled to do what they like with it." Had not the Shah himself bought property in Switzerland? In any case the people concerned were only following the example of the members of the royal family, who owned any amount of property in Europe and the U.S.

The high cost of living, the often exorbitant profit margins of Iranian enterprises, and widespread fiscal fraud—all these were enriching the "new" upper middle class at the expense of the lower middle and working classes. The compulsory sale of forty-nine percent of shares to the workers upset and annoyed the bosses.

In May 1977 the new United States ambassador, William H. Sullivan, took part in a businessmen's seminar in New York. In the course of the discussions it was concluded that there was only a very slim chance of Iran transforming itself from an oil-based economy to a broadly industrialized state; those present considered that Iran lacked the material and human infrastructure necessary to support the advanced military and industrial technology imported by the Shah. The seminar even advised the ambassador to speak frankly to the Shah, at the risk of becoming *persona non grata*.*

* *New York Times,* May 30, 1977.

To the ordinary Iranian, the deterioration of the economy in his daily life meant frequent power cuts, food shortages and the growth of the black market.

The One-Party State and Nonparticipation

But even more than the chaotic state of the economy, it was the absence of any popular participation in the decision-making process which explains the unanimous revolt against the Shah's regime. No section of society and no sphere of life was free from the sovereign's control. His shadow lay across the entire country. The result was a general feeling of alienation. On February 9, 1975, I wrote in my diary: "I resent nonparticipation to such a degree that all coherent thought deserts me. . . . Everything seems bogus. Impression that we are all phantoms jostling about on the proscenium in front of an unreal stage set. The feeling of identification with a homeland in progress, which moved me once, is quickly fading. We are actors in a tragicomedy with no certain outcome."

The dissolution of political parties and the creation of the single Rastakhiz party in 1975 was practically the last straw. Many responsible people, including my brother, were agreed that the Shah was making a big mistake, but such was his ascendancy that everyone gave way.

The monarch saw his single party as a means of channeling discontent and giving any critics the chance to make themselves heard in a context safely under his personal supervision. It was also intended to be an instrument for the political education of the people. But the party was run from the top downward; it had no popular roots. Iranians were invited to rally round it, and they did so, but only because they were afraid of calling attention to themselves if they did otherwise. I have a clear memory of the Foreign Ministry's instructions in this matter. I was sent a register in which to enter the names of any of the embassy staff who "wished" to join. All of them signed their names, silently, and with glum expressions. But in private they expressed their displeasure.

Certainly to the Shah's way of thinking he was promoting a kind of "guided," gradual democracy. But what was the use of compulsory loyalty, reluctantly given? The public wanted participation in decisions; all the Shah had to offer was the chance to debate the ways of implementing "his" revolution, not the basis of the country's problems. His definition of participation was at odds with the people's.

Jamshid Amuzegar, twice the party's general secretary, told the *Wall Street Journal* on November 4, 1977, that with Iran's population standing at thirty-four million, and likely to double in twenty-five to thirty years, the Shah considered that no one man could govern sixty million people on his own, and that the people would have to learn how to participate in government. The journalist asked why the people could not be permitted to start playing their part right now, and Amuzegar explained that fifty-five percent of the population was illiterate; if you gave responsibility to illiterates who knew nothing about the affairs of government, you would end with nothing but disorder and anarchy. This contemptuous elitism naturally caused the "lower" classes to thoroughly loathe their "betters."

On top of that, whereas the Shah promised freedom of debate inside his single party, at the same time he said that he did not want any opposition. These contradictions further weakened an organization which had no real popular support in the first place. It was hardly surprising that there was rumbling unrest in almost every field. All Iran's foreign visitors admitted the material development of the country, but they also stressed the lack of enthusiasm and participation.

On September 26, 1975, I wrote to a friend: "The big problem in Iran right now is not economic but cultural. A cultural substructure loosely and imperfectly bound to a Western veneer will not hold. The country is heading for disaster. The more the material side is assured, the more the metaphysical problems will grow."

Totally neglecting the intellectuals when it was not actually harassing them, the regime promoted general mediocrity. The Ministry of Culture, under the authority of the Shah's own brother-in-law, stifled all creative thinking. As for the cultural activities of the Empress, despite the goodwill she invested in them they did not affect the masses. Referring to the Museum of Modern Art created by the Shahbanou in 1977 under the directorship of her cousin, the critic André Fermigier wrote:

> Rather than chasing after a West which itself is desperately in pursuit of its own folklore and a picture-postcard primitivism, some countries would do better to integrate their own past, and before setting off into the blue they should synthesize what they already have.

. . . That the oil-producing countries are becoming big importers of works of art is undoubtedly a boon for certain galleries. Iranian painting will be none the better for it.*

Censorship and the gagging of writers did anything but encourage the opening out of Iranian society. It drove the intellectual elite into the ranks of the opposition.

Religious Unrest

As I was walking through the bazaar in Yazd in the spring of 1971 I noticed some small posters announcing: "The return of the [hidden] Imam is at hand." Those words struck me as a warning, but, wrapped in his own aloofness, the Shah paid little attention to the accumulating signs. Unlike Sadat, he never set foot in a mosque to pray alongside the faithful.

In any case the relations of the clergy with the regime had never been cordial. Even in the Shah's father's time, the religious establishment was never handled with any great care. Once, he entered the tomb of Fatima in Qom without taking his boots off, and physically bullied the mullahs who dared to criticize him.

The Shah curiously underestimated the influence of the priesthood. When Olivier Warin asked him if he still had difficulties with the mullahs he replied, "Perhaps they grumble now and then, but it has no effect."

* *Le Monde*, October 27, 1977.

Then he claimed that Khomeini had no following in Iran: "Nobody cares about him here, except for terrorists; the so-called Islamic Marxists may sometimes speak his name, but that's all." He went on to say, "That tradition . . . of mullahs keeping knowledge to themselves so as to maintain their hold on power has now completely disappeared."*

Remarks like that sound surprising today, particularly in view of the amount of criticism of the regime which was going on in the Koranic schools and in the mosques. And Khomeini was continuing his teaching from his exile in Najaf; a good many theology students were paying him secret visits and returning to spread his message in Iran.

But even outside purely religious circles the Islamic movement was an important political influence from the mid-1960s onward. Thus Ali Shariati, professor of sociology at the University of Mashhad, by bringing Shi'ite thinking up to date and putting it at the service of the revolutionary and anti-imperialist struggle had created a tide of enthusiasm among students all over the country.

The fact is that discontent had never abated in religious circles since the tragic events of 1963 that resulted in the exile of Khomeini, and all those with visions of overthrowing the regime made sure to consult the ayatollahs. Thus, in 1967 Teymur Bakhtiar, the founder of SAVAK, visited Iraq to contact Khomeini. He was helped by the Iraqi authorities, who were at loggerheads with the Shah at the time. But SAVAK agents succeeded in assassinating him.

* Olivier Warin, *Le Lion et le soleil.*

Nevertheless it is fair to say that it was religious unrest which sounded the death knell of the regime. It was under the banner of Shi'ism that the Iranian people mustered the energy and solidarity necessary to bring down the Pahlavi dictatorship. It was religion that gave the masses the strength to stop living normal lives during the long months of strikes and hardships.

Their religion counted, but so did their youth. In 1977 nearly half the population was under sixteen, and two thirds under thirty. Young people were the backbone of the demonstrators who stood up to an over-equipped army with their bare hands.

This blend of religion and youth deserves the utmost attention, because that is what got the better of the Shah. Anyone who recalls the crucial role of martyrdom in Shi'ism will understand that "dying power" is a far more formidable force than "killing power." This is what the French philosopher André Glucksmann has to say on the subject:

> Contrary to the common view, the greatest power . . . does not come out of a gun, but out of readiness to suffer death. Dying power, which is also a collective power, embraces kinds of knowledge . . . which are the means by which peoples, cultures and civilizations cohere and communicate. . . . In the long run that dying power changes the world; that is what constitutes the strength of social movements, not the killing power of the military. . . .*

These words apply with peculiar relevance to the increasingly vast gatherings that commemorated the vic-

* *Le Nouvel Observateur*, June 11, 1979.

tims of the demonstrations in Tehran every forty days starting in January 1978.

The International Situation

Foreign policy was another of the Shah's private domains. He feared the Soviet Union more than anything else. In 1970 he was worried by the rapprochement between India and the USSR. When the Indo–Pakistani war led to the creation of Bangladesh in 1971 he no longer doubted that our northern neighbor had in mind some vast encircling movement against Iran. This idea turned into an obsession after 1972, and it explains his efforts to transform the country into a military power at full speed. That is why he remained deaf to counsels of moderation.

The sovereign's anxiety is understandable if you take heed of the fact that Iran has always been a theater for foreign intrigues. It was a British preserve until the Second World War, after coming under heavy Russian pressure in the north in the days of the tsars. During the Second World War the British agreed with the Russians to occupy Iran, which was a natural route for supplying arms for the Red Army. In those days I was a student at the Lycée Français in Beirut. In 1941, after the abdication of Reza Shah, several of his children arrived in Lebanon to pursue their studies. One of them, Ahmad Reza, gave an account of his father's reaction one day while I was there. Apparently the British had promised to allow him to take up residence in India, but when the ship arrived off Bombay he was informed that he was to be dispatched to South Africa. The old Shah flew into a towering rage, swearing and thundering, "I always knew that the British were not to be trusted!"

The influence of foreign powers was such that even to this day there are many Iranians who believe that the Shah's fall would not have been possible without them. Obviously they have in mind the CIA-orchestrated coup of 1953, which led to the overthrow of the Mossadeq government. Certainly the Shah's intemperate statements and arrogant criticism of the West in his latter years was a source of vexation for the Western leaderships. It is equally obvious that he had alienated the big oil companies by his hawkish role in OPEC. Again it is understandable that with his ill-considered purchases of arms he disturbed his neighbors, and especially the Soviet Union. But to go on from there to infer the existence of one or several foreign plots is rather a long step. It may be that both sides encouraged the dissidents of the left or the right. (Though it is certainly true that the human-rights policy inaugurated by Carter drew some opponents out of cover.) I do not believe that the Shah's close advisers, and particularly the American ambassador, whom he saw every day, made any deliberate attempt to induce mistakes. The Shah made enough on his own.

Nevertheless there are those who maintain that the Iranian revolution was only the first installment of a vast plan intended to destabilize the entire region. I shall come back to this theory later on.

Be that as it may, as I have already pointed out, the

Shah's "policy of national independence" had established a relative balance of power between the two superpowers, and gained him real credibility. In 1971 his recognition of the People's Republic of China and his establishment of relations with Cuba and East Germany gave further credence to his foreign policy. But from 1972–73 onward things changed, and the balance was broken.

As usual, and without bothering to explain his motives to those close to him, let alone his people, the Shah suddenly decided to extend his perimeter of defense, to intervene against the revolutionaries in Dhofar, and to back Somalia against the USSR. And at the very moment when black Africa was starting to carry some weight on the international scene he chose to strengthen his relationship with South Africa. How often I drew his attention to the dismal consequences of that policy, both in my reports and when we met. He would not listen. His arrogance toward the Arabs was equally vexing. Having spent my childhood in Arab countries, not only did I see no difference between us, but I also felt a deep cultural bond.

Once I even tried to get a word in about Amnesty International. That was in 1970. It made him furious with me. "They're Communists!" he snapped. But when the shooting of unarmed men became a slaughter I returned to the attack, and with the help of my brother I managed to have the gates opened for Martin Ennals.

When Ardeshir Zahedi's extravagant diplomatic receptions brought a critical response from the American press in 1976, the Shah told me during an audience, "We don't know whether they're harmful or not. In any case Zahedi has all the American senators in his pocket." What could I say in reply to a judgment like that?

But let us come back to the present. As if to provoke the Soviet Union, on April 7, 1978, the Shah raised a great commotion in announcing the destruction of a spy network belonging to our northern neighbor. A few weeks later an old retired general faced the firing squad for his involvement in this affair. Why make such a gesture at a time when our domestic problems were worsening? The republican *coup d'état* in Afghanistan alarmed the Shah and revived his fears of encirclement by the Soviet Union.

A usually well-informed person considered that this espionage business had been used to put pressure on the Congress of the United States. Many senators were opposed to the sale of aircraft equipped with the AWACS system (an ultrasophisticated electronic detection method) to Iran, for fear that it would fall into Soviet hands. The Shah wanted to show them how efficiently his counterespionage services were working.

Taking into consideration the slogans of the demonstrators, it has to be admitted that foreign-policy changes did exert some influence on the fall of the regime. Certainly there is no doubt that outside forces did attempt to take advantage of domestic discontent, if only through propaganda. The Libyan and PLO leaderships abused the Shah, and the pro-Communist Radio Peyké Iran criticized his recent policy. As for the Western press and nongovernmental organizations, they campaigned against political repression. Obviously the various secret services were also at work behind the scenes.

But there is no smoke without fire: the crisis originated right inside the country, and, as this brief glance back over the latter years of the regime has shown, the elements necessary for the overthrow of the dynasty were coming together. The change could well have come in 1953. The *coup d'état* arranged by the CIA only postponed the day.

Tehran, July 1978

My brother was dining with some friends when he was called to the telephone. On the orders of one of the Shah's sisters, the Imperial Guard had just seized her foreign partner in a deal to build a block of flats. Feeling that this partner had done her wrong, the princess had not bothered to follow legal process, but had simply taken that role on herself. The partner had been handed over to the police, and in order to be released he had to pay the princess a million dollars.

After numerous telephone calls my brother returned to his hosts, sank into an armchair, and murmured, "The regime is dying inside."

Yes, the regime was doomed, and to understand its rapid downfall it will help to become better acquainted with the man who embodied it. In one sense the Shah was really the architect of his own defeat. The evolution of his character will make that clear.

3

_ THE CHANGING SHAH _

In my own country I already hold the supreme
rank and power dependent upon the law and
upon the special spiritual ties which bind me
to my people.

—Mohammad Reza Pahlavi, *Towards the Great
Civilization*

The setting sun gilded the columns of the palace of Persepolis. Guards dressed as Achaemenid warriors with their curled hair and beards were lining the great double stairway, their lances flashing. Around the Shah and the Shahbanou, kings, presidents and prime ministers clustered on the huge rostrum erected at the foot of the famous ruins.

A company of horsemen had set out from Tehran the previous day, and now it rode up to the dais and its captain dismounted to present a handwritten parchment to the sovereign. The nation's message of homage. Snug in his ornate uniform, the Shah replied, his flat voice projected over the waiting crowd by an elaborate loudspeaker system:

"Hail to the great and noble Iranian people, creator and builder of our glorious history.

"Hail, Cyrus, founder of the Persian Empire and immortal hero of human history . . .

"On this historic day when the whole country renews its allegiance to its glorious past, I, Shahanshah of Iran, call history to witness that we, the heirs of Cyrus, have kept the promise made two thousand five hundred years ago. We have remained loyal to our mission, we have made our culture an instrument of peace and love. . . .

"Darius, great King of Kings, proclaimed in an inscription still visible on these walls: 'Let this realm be forever shielded from evil and falsehood; let right and justice be its eternal guides; let the stronger be able to mistreat the weaker no more; let no man be permitted to do harm to others. . . .' "

These last words of the Shahanshah, Light of the Aryans, second in line of the Pahlavi dynasty, were lost in the opening chords of the hymn to the monarchy. Now came an incredible parade of imperial warriors from different eras of the country's past: a prehistoric fighting man, Achaemenid "Immortals," a wheeled siege tower, a trireme in full sail, Parthian horsemen, Sassanid archers, Safavid infantry, modern units, and then representatives of the "armies" of development. The audience might have been dreaming: it was as if some Technicolor epic of Cecil B. de Mille's were being projected onto the screen of the vast plain.

The previous day at Pasargadae, before the empty tomb of Cyrus, the Shah had intoned:

"To you, Cyrus, Great King, King of Kings, from Myself, Shahanshah of Iran, and from my people, hail!

". . . We are here at this moment when Iran renews its pledge to history to bear witness to the immense gratitude of an entire people to you, immortal hero of history, founder of the world's oldest empire, great liberator of all time, worthy son of mankind.

"Cyrus, we stand before your eternal dwelling place to speak these solemn words: Sleep on in peace forever, for we are watching, and we shall remain to watch over your glorious heritage."

With the parade over, the illustrious guests followed their imperial host into the sumptuous tented village built and decorated by French experts. Millions of dollars had been spent on housing and feeding the attending heads of state and other dignitaries. In Iran, outside the sovereigns' immediate entourage and the career sycophants, criticism seethed, but was expressed only by discreet remarks in the privacy of people's homes. Abroad, the press had a field day. How could a developing country dig so deep into its purse to put on some sort of "fancy-dress party" or at least a *son et lumière* show, instead of devoting its money to improving its people's standard of living? (The same sort of criticisms broke out all over the world seven years later, on the occasion of the coronation of Bokassa the First, Emperor of Central Africa.)

The Shah blustered that his expenditure had not been unproductive. It had speeded up the implementation of the national programs—more schools, village electrification, extension of roads and telecommunications, and so on. Anyway, the tents would remain and would come in useful on other occasions. And what about the prestige of the country? Didn't that count? For three days Persepolis had become an international capital where heads of state had met and had often settled their problems. But above all, the Iranian people had remembered their glorious past.

Appointment with History

Mohammad Reza Pahlavi insisted to all comers on the profound meaning of the festivities which testified to the vitality of the new Iran, heir and upholder of the empire of the Achaemenids. It was a case of restoring the faith of the people by reminding them of their history. "Not only does our white revolution draw its inspiration from the reign of Cyrus," he told his entourage, "but it also engenders parallels with it." He intended to make the celebration of twenty-five centuries of monarchy the signal for the rebirth of the whole country. By leading his people to this real appointment with their own history he was seeking to imbue them with the spirituality of ancient Iran.

Yet oddly enough the people were absent from the ceremonies, kept at arm's length by police and Army on the great plain of Persepolis. Furthermore, this return to "source" antagonized the clergy who knew no other law than the teaching of the Prophet of Islam.

Interviewed by the Indian journalist R. K. Karanjia, the Shah said:

> "Today our ancient land, the mother of civilization, which gave the world its first empire, is in the throes of a glorious rebirth. Our White Revolution has its roots in a similar bloodless revolution that was accomplished by the Emperor Cyrus some 2500 years ago, when he built his empire and within a single generation welded it into

a cultural and socioeconomic entity which was to establish an entirely new pattern of moral, humanistic, civilized life and values."

Karanjia then asked the sovereign, "Would it then be correct to conclude that the Cyrus festival heralded something like a renaissance—that is, a rediscovery and resurrection of Iran's lost Aryan ethos?" The Shah replied:

"It was certainly a rediscovery and a renaissance, but why do you say 'lost' ethos? Really, Iran never lost it. For despite setbacks, reverses, even national calamities, the legacy of Cyrus, this flaming Aryan torch of ours, has been kept alight and passed on through our history, from generation to generation, linking the past with the present and ensuring the future."*

The Shah redoubled these references to Iran's Aryan roots after 1971, both in speeches and in the interviews he gave. In *Towards the Great Civilization*, published in 1977, he went so far as to say:

Iranian civilization, of which the Great Civilization will be the most accomplished form, is an outstanding manifestation of Aryan civilization. . . . Its progress toward perfection has never ceased. . . . If our race has constantly sought its way in the Aryan civilization, it is because its creative genius is indissolubly linked to its fundamental principles. Darius the Great, by describing himself as Aryan and the son of an Aryan, Iranian and the son of an Iranian, in fact refers to the numerous qualities which reflect the adjectives Aryan and Iranian.

* Quotes from R. K. Karanjia, *The Mind of a Monarch* (London: Allen & Unwin, 1977), pp. 1–3.

. . . This civilization is based in its deepest sense upon life and creativity. Within it, light constitutes the highest manifestation of Creation, for all beauty and all creative strength derive their origin from it.

Reading this book, some of whose accents recall another dictator who saw his empire crumble, the mind boggles. It also wonders how the Shah managed to overlook his people's powerful attachment to the Islamic faith. These references to pre-Islamic beliefs became more and more numerous during the final years of his reign, and they were bound to alarm the Shi'ite clergy. The last straw came in 1977, when the sovereign altered the calendar to start not with the Hegira but with the foundation of the Persian Empire by Cyrus the Great.

The Obsession with Legitimacy

It may be that the Shah genuinely believed in the virtues of the Aryan race and values. His remarks on this subject nevertheless remain rationalizations in the psychoanalytic sense of the word, which conceal deeper drives. What he was seeking was to legitimate himself by building a bridge between himself and the great kings of the past. This need for legitimacy had possessed him for a long time, judging by the pomp and ceremony he required around himself. The idea of the Persepolis celebrations went back to the early 1960s. He saw them as establishing the continuity of Iranian history and the unbroken line of the monarchy in the eyes of the great of this world. For who else were all these heads of state, presidents or monarchs of today but the representatives of countries with a relatively recent history? Whereas he, Mohammad Reza Pahlavi, was the heir of Cyrus the Great! His own father had meant to connect the new dynasty with distant ancestors years before when he had adopted the patronym "Pahlavi."

In order to understand this consuming need, one has only to go back to the Shah's origins. He was only seven years old when Reza Khan had himself crowned emperor. The family came from very humble beginnings. There is a story that at one point in his childhood his father was a herdsman. But the Shah dreamed up a more glamorous genealogy. He traced his ancestors back to the clan of the Bavands, inhabitants of the High Mazandaran, cradle of the ancient Iranian races, and he described his grandfather and great-grandfather as officers of "the old Persian Army."

In fact Reza Khan was of poor extraction, and the Shah preferred to remain rather vague about his family's history before the engagement of his father in the Persian Cossack Brigade at the age of fifteen. After being promoted to lieutenant in 1916, Reza Khan married the daughter of a prosperous landowner, and when her husband's star ascended she obtained him the title of Taj el Moluk (Crown of Kings) from the last Qajar king. Later on she said of Reza Khan, "His parents were simple farmers and he had no education. Thanks to a ferocious will, after joining the Army as a completely illiterate private he climbed the ladder of the military hierarchy step by step."[*]

* *Confidences*, Paris, No. 1094 (1968).

When Reza Khan entered Tehran in 1921 at the head of the garrison of Qazvin to kick out the Prime Minister of the day, he was wearing a colonel's uniform. Ahmad Shah Qajar made him a general and granted him the title of Sardar Sepah (Chief of the Army). Once on the throne, he confiscated a number of estates and so became one of the country's biggest landowners. Aristocracy was measured in acres in those days; through those seizures no doubt he too was attempting to legitimate himself. But as a career soldier he continued to lead a relatively frugal life.

His son, probably feeling his father's humble origins only too keenly, wanted to be indisputably noble. In an aristocratic gesture he shared out the land his father had acquired among the peasants who worked on it. He strove to establish his authority and made a great point of national celebrations: in 1965 the twenty-fifth anniversary of his reign (on which occasion he had Parliament confer upon him the title of Aryamehr, Light of the Aryans); in 1967 his coronation; in 1969 the thirtieth anniversary of his reign; in 1971 the 2500th anniversary of national monarchy; in 1976 the fiftieth anniversary of the Pahlavi dynasty, and so on.

With the celebrations at Persepolis he presented himself to the assembled heads of state as the heir to the founder of the Persian Empire. The continuity of Iranian history was personified in the Shah. At long last he was legitimate.

Nowadays many people say that the deep change in the sovereign's personality dates from those celebrations, which drew attention to the luxury and extravagance of the Iranian court. What most amazes me, as I often remarked at the time, is that the Shah had no need whatever of those costly celebrations to reinforce his authority. The fact is that he had already won his legitimacy through his development program, whose first fruits were already impressing both the world and his people. In less than seven years his country had emerged from its backward state, poverty was disappearing, factories were springing up, the peasants had become landowners, unemployment had declined and the national income was growing. You had only to travel around the country to realize the deep changes which were slowly but surely transforming the entire tissue of society. That he was determined to have himself crowned is understandable. That he should have waited for twenty-six years before doing it can also be accepted. He himself put forward an apparently logical explanation: that he had waited for his people's standard of living to improve. Was that not a form of legitimation? The coronation followed as a consequence of services rendered, because the people recognized what might be called the utility of the sovereign, and so offered him the crown. Actually he could then have created a new line rooted in tradition: to have the crown given to him by a representative of the people, and not to take it himself. A true leader should be chosen or elected.

Instead of all that ceremonial it would undoubtedly have been a wiser move to highlight the festivities for the 2500th anniversary of the monarchy by democratizing the country's institutions. In the early 1970s the material and social successes of the regime made liberalization perfectly possible. When he fell back on pomp and ceremony Mohammad Reza Pahlavi, Light of the Aryans, missed his appointment with his own people.

In basing his legitimacy on the distant past he began to cut himself off from the realities of the present.

My First Meeting with the Shah

I first met the Shah in Paris in August 1948, during an official visit. He still looked very young, and reminded me of the shy adolescent I had glimpsed in 1938 when he stopped at Beirut on his way to Cairo to marry King Farouk's sister, Princess Fawzia. I then occupied a minor post as attaché to our Paris embassy, and since I knew the language I was entrusted with all the more thankless tasks: accompanying visitors to the airport, discussing economic affairs with the Quai d'Orsay, writing correspondence, telephoning dinner menus to caterers, and so on. A week before the sovereign's arrival, Ambassador Ali Soheyli, a veteran politician and former prime minister, summoned me to his office. "The Shah is like his late father," he told me, "very sensitive to coverage in the press. You remember how before the war two articles in *L'Os à moëlle* and *Le Canard enchaîné*, the satirical papers, produced a diplomatic split with France? Well, I want you to go and see all the newspapers to avoid any ill-timed jokes."

So I set to work. The job did not seem too hard, because in those days there was no SAVAK and Iran was not a page-one lead for the dailies. Also I had friends in most editorial offices. But the left-wing press was not especially fond of the Shah, whose government had dissolved all Iran's progressive political groupings following the collapse of the short-lived Republic of Azerbaijan, set up in the north in 1945 before the Soviet Union withdrew its forces of occupation. I didn't know anybody on *Le Canard enchainé*, but a friend in the French Foreign Ministry took the matter in hand. *Le Canard* contented itself with a few lines which I quote from memory: "The phone rings: an important personage warns us against any irreverence toward the imperial guest. When we protest against this infringement of freedom of speech he asks us whether we don't own cars and go away for weekends. 'Doesn't Persia remind you of anything?' he asks. 'What about oil?' Fatherlike he advises us to think how much gasoline we need!" (At that time there was fuel rationing in France.)

The Shah did not seem very sure of himself in those days. His entourage, though deferential, passed remarks to him. The ambassador observed protocol but treated him rather like a child. Outwardly very shy, he listened attentively and in moments of hesitation cast desperate glances toward familiar faces. He had one or two evenings free, and spent them in nightclubs in the company of call girls procured by his friends. He loaded these girls with sumptuous gifts. At a reception held a few months later I met a young lady who had spent time with the Shah. She proudly displayed the diamond he had given her.

When he ascended the throne in 1941 his father's departure had opened the floodgates and the politicians and clergy had surged back in. They surrounded the young monarch with their advice, and took care to keep him in a purely honorific position. Free elections produced a majority for the feudalists and their allies, and they meant to have their way. The Shah resented this situation, but could do nothing about it.

Iran was run by the British. It was receiving a pittance for its oil, and was totally destitute. The occupation of the country by the British in the south and the Russians in the north had recreated the situation which had existed before the First World War. The ministers chosen by Parliament were all well-known figures who valued their links with the big powers and kept the Shah under close supervision.

The young sovereign was suffocating. He needed some brilliant stroke which would enable him to improve his public image and regain confidence in himself. The opportunity arose with the Azerbaijan question. The Russians were in no hurry to evacuate the province, where an autonomous pro-Soviet regime had been established. Thanks to American pressure the Russians eventually withdrew, whereupon the Shah took command of the Army in person, and reoccupied the region in 1947.

From the Assassination Attempt in 1949 to the Fall of Mossadeq

In 1949 he won his badge of courage. At the university opening ceremony a press photographer came up to the monarch and fired several shots at him, grazing his cheek, ear and shoulder. The Shah had a miraculous escape from death, as he escaped it years later, in 1965, when a guard turned his automatic weapon on him. This gave birth to the twin legends of his "indomitable courage" and his "divine protection."

In the Shah's entourage there were some who reckoned that the supremacy of Parliament, with its shifting majorities and powerless governments, was favorable to a Communist advance. These people took advantage of the incident to encourage the sovereign to follow in his father's footsteps and make a bid for personal power. They blamed the parties of the left for the attempted assassination and grabbed the opportunity to ban them. The feudal interest were exhorted to line up with the Shah so as to put an end to "subversion." Britain and its oil company, the Anglo-Iranian Oil Company (AIOC), whose contract was due to expire, played their trump card, the King, because only he was capable of getting the concession renewed.

The Shah, for his part, did his best to rally the Army behind him. Early in 1950 he seemed to be master of the situation. But negotiations between the government and the AIOC were going through a critical phase, principally over the question of increasing the royalties paid by the company to the government. In Parliament a nationalist group led by Dr. Mohammad Mossadeq criticized these dealings and called for the nationalization of the oil fields. By publicizing what was at stake in the negotiations, as well as the intrigues of the AIOC, Mossadeq raised a storm of protest, especially in the bazaar. At the same time the Shi'ite clergy feared a return to the state of affairs that had existed in Reza Shah's time. Armed with his new authority, the Shah summoned to power General Razmara, the strong man of the Army. A few months later, on March 7, 1951, a fanatic shot and killed the General while he was attending a funeral at the Shah Mosque. The Shah at once replaced him with one of his supporters, Hussein Ala. When the agitation threatened to go on growing, he eventually caved in to pressure and appointed Mossadeq prime minister, even though he detested him. (I was present on several occasions when he described Mossadeq as a "stooge" in the pay of the British.)

Mossadeq forced Parliament to vote unanimously in favor of oil nationalization and made the Shah sign the new law, producing a wave of enthusiasm throughout the country. His colorful personality, frequent fainting fits, and habit of receiving the most important guests while lying in bed in his pajamas won him great popularity. Édouard Herriot remarked of Mossadeq at the time, "He's in perfect ill health" (*Il possède une mauvaise santé de fer*).

Some Iranian observers were skeptical, considering that foreign interests were pulling the strings: top-ranking non-British companies on the world market were pushing for a breaking of the contract with the AIOC. Be that as it may, when the nationalist uproar grew the Iranian ruling class and various foreign powers got the wind up and turned to the Shah again. It was then that the CIA floated the idea of a *coup d'état*, and in 1953 Kermit Roosevelt visited Tehran to examine the possibilities and find a likely candidate. He found his man in General Fazlollah Zahedi, and the plotters staged the departure of the Shah after having him sign a decree naming Zahedi prime minister. He used CIA money to buy the services of Shaban-bi-mokh (literally, Shaban the Scatterbrain), the master of a famous *zurkhané* (a traditional gymnastics club), in order to recruit a commando squad of "civilians" to act in concert with the Army. The operation, in August 1953, did not take more than a day, and then the Shah made a triumphal return. And the very people who had followed Mossadeq right up to the eleventh hour scurried to the airport and prostrated themselves before the sovereign to kiss his boots.

In spite of the facts, which have been disclosed by the Americans themselves, the Shah was pleased to consider the 1953 coup a "popular revolution" which gave him the mandate of the people. And apparently he ended up believing his own propaganda. Already the sovereign was showing a tendency to bend the truth; it was to intensify to the point of cutting him right off from the realities of the country.

Toward Dictatorship

But the Shah's triumph in 1953 left something to be desired. It was not total. Fazlollah Zahedi got to be a nuisance. Corruption flourished once again, and repression, particularly of the Communists in the Tudeh party, reached unimaginable heights. Furthermore, the Shah found himself in many respects back on the leash—a situation which did not suit him at all. He tried to get rid of his Prime Minister. At this juncture the General's son Ardeshir, who had himself played an important part in the preparation and execution of the coup, fell in love with Princess Shahnaz, the Shah's daughter by Fawzia. His father encouraged the romance, they married, and the Shah took advantage of the situation to appoint his son-in-law ambassador to Washington, replacing Ali Amini.

General Zahedi had developed a heart defect. He was invited to resign and was replaced by one of the court flunkeys, Dr. Eqbal, who signed all his missives to the sovereign by describing himself as *gholamé jan nessar* ("slave ready to sacrifice his life"). An irreverent public nicknamed him Gholamé Halgheh Bégouch ("slave with a ring through his ear").

General Zahedi became his country's permanent representative at the office of the United Nations in Geneva. He did not grumble—he liked Geneva and its nearby casinos. The Shah bought him an estate of his own where he could gather his friends around him, and he never set foot in the Palais des Nations except on the day he presented his credentials. (His appointment illustrates one of the typical features of the regime: the use of official posts to remove or reward people for services rendered.)

Of course his father's dismissal annoyed Ardeshir. A friend who wants to remain anonymous reported the following incident to me: One evening Ardeshir got drunk. He insulted the Shah in front of several people by calling him an "ingrate." My friend says that Ardeshir added that he had documents damaging to the Shah stowed away in a Swiss bank and would bring them out at the proper time.

Meanwhile the country's economic situation continued to deteriorate. After Mossadeq, oil exploitation had been handed over to a consortium of Western companies, and now it was paying better than it had before (fifty percent of the profits). But corruption and incompetence were a constant drain on the country's revenue. Once again Iran found itself on the verge of bankruptcy.

The new richer class clashed with the power of the feudal landowners. Real-estate speculation was creating an unhealthy atmosphere. The state was surviving only because of American subsidies. In the absence of banks, businessmen short of liquid cash borrowed from the merchants in the bazaar at prohibitive rates of interest. Unemployment grew. Social and political unrest increased. In this situation, and under pressure from the Americans, who promised him further aid, the Shah placed the government in the hands of Ali Amini. Amini had no intention of leaving the real power to the Shah. His Agriculture Minister, Arsanjani, worked out the first steps toward agricultural reform. This only incurred the hostility of the big landowners and property speculators. Amini did not last long. He was replaced by a faithful supporter of the Shah, Assadollah Alam.

From then onward the way to dictatorship was clear. All it took was keeping the key posts away from anybody with a mind of his own. The Shah worked out a hasty program of reforms, much of it based on previous studies by the Amini Cabinet. The "old establishment" in his entourage and in the government now reckoned him rather too "revolutionary" and warned him against any rapid modernization, whereupon the Shah simply eliminated them by sending them into retirement.

In 1963 the clergy and the merchants in the bazaar

tried to foment a rebellion, but it was bloodily repressed. Khomeini, who had encouraged the rioting against land reform, was arrested and then exiled. In the south of the country the chief of the Kashkai tribe led his men against the Army, but was defeated and took the road to exile in his own turn.

Now the Shah was safely home. His reform program was approved by referendum with a majority of over ninety-five percent. To avoid any possibility of a comeback by the "old establishment" the sovereign entrusted the government to a team of young technocrats led by Hassan Ali Mansour.

The Shah neutralized every political or social group that stood in his way. He eliminated all likely freethinkers from the Army, and relied like all dictators on a powerful, loyal Army, a brutal secret police, a political elite kept well under his thumb, and a bureaucracy preoccupied with technocracy.

Thus he destroyed all valid representation of other viewpoints. He removed all possible rivals at every level, and muzzled intellectuals, politicians, the press, Parliament—the whole people, in fact.

His absolute power was undisputed from then on, but since he had a progressive program and the means to carry it out, most people gave him, if not their trust, then at least the benefit of the doubt. Actually he appeared not to be abusing his authority at first, and behaved like an absolute but "enlightened" monarch. I twice met him in France during that spectacular recovery.

My Second and Third Meetings with the Shah

I saw the Shah for the second time in 1959, when he visited France at the invitation of General de Gaulle. At that time I had been away from the Foreign Ministry for some years and was working at UNESCO, but I found myself doubly involved in the ceremonies occasioned by the royal visit. First, at the request of our ambassador, Nasrollah Entezam, I drafted a number of outlines for speeches by the sovereign. Second, as vice-president of the Franco-Iranian Association I was invited to the dinners. One day I had to accompany the French members of the Association's steering committee to the audience granted by the Shah. He did not recognize me, of course, and shook hands with me and spoke to me in French, as he did to everybody else. I refrained from disclosing my identity. The Shah launched into a discussion about the importance of cultural relations between France and Iran, and as we were leaving he turned to Entezam and said to him in Persian, in a smug voice, "I really had them going with my remarks about culture, didn't I?"

My third meeting with the Shah dates back to 1962, when he came to Paris to open the exhibition Seven Thousand Years of Iranian Art. On that occasion he was accompanied by the Empress Farah. I was presented to him by the director general of UNESCO as an Iranian official of that organization, and had to sit through the speech I had written for him. I also attended the dinner he gave in honor of General and Madame de Gaulle, but did not speak to him. Compared with the two previous meetings, I thought, he looked a lot more sure of himself. Since I was following the country's affairs only from a distance, I had no idea as yet that he was getting ready to carry out his reforms and was about to establish his full authority over the government. But the way he behaved denoted a great change in his general style.

After going back to the Foreign Ministry I saw him often, both at private receptions and in official audiences. In spite of his status as uncontested leader he still remained open to argument, and could even be quite affable. But at the start of the 1970s a change took place in the Shah's character, and at the end of his reign his true nature was to surface once again.

The Court in 1965

The Shah believed in his "White Revolution." When I met him a few days after my arrival in Tehran in February 1965 he sounded convincing as he told me, "We must all forget our past disagreements and close ranks to rescue the country from underdevelopment and ensure a bright future for later generations." He was sitting on a marble table in his sister Princess Ashraf's villa, with his hands beneath his thighs and his legs dangling. "I am going to go faster than the left," he promised. "You're all going to have to run to keep up with me. All the old economic and political feudalism is over and done with. Everybody should benefit directly from the product of his own labor. That's the objective of my agrarian reforms. And for the workers we shall institute profit sharing." He stood up to rejoin his partners at bridge, and added, "All young people must come back and take part in our great work." He was talking much the same language as any Communist leader.

In those days Princess Ashraf had made something of a specialty of recruiting leftists and bringing them back to the fold. On their side they were frustrated by years of inaction and believed like everyone else in the stability of the regime, seeing that it was supported by the West and lately wooed by the East as well. They saw no alternative to joining in the movement in the hope of democratizing it from within.

Life at court was still tinged with a certain simplicity. The Shah's brothers and sisters gave buffet dinners which were no different from the receptions given by any well-to-do member of the middle class in the capital or in other towns elsewhere in the world. After the meal some people played cards and others watched films. I might add that these showed a fairly lowbrow taste; as a former critic for *Cahiers du cinéma* I was surprised by the Shah's partiality for cloak-and-dagger adventures or Louis de Funès comedies.

One evening there was a showing of the Costa-Gavras film *Z*, a fictionalized version of the Greek colonels' coup. I believe it was at Princess Fatima's house (her husband was the head of the Air Force). Within half an hour the incensed Shah had the show stopped. Of course the film never reached the public screen, and the distributor barely avoided getting into bad trouble.

At these receptions guests would often arrive with files of documents under their arms. They waited for the sovereign to send for them, spent a few minutes with him in private, and emerged with beaming expressions, presumably armed with the authorizations they needed. I was constantly amazed by this perfunctory manner of conducting state business.

Despite an outward display of unity there was no love lost between the members of the royal family, who were not all children of the same mother. Inside court circles they sniped at each other more or less openly, and I often observed their backbiting at parties, with amusement to begin with, but later with dismay at the thought of the way their rivalries affected the affairs of the country. Every prince and princess kept a small court and a larger entourage, and ill-feeling proliferated among their courtiers like the ripples from a thrown pebble.

As for business, originally the princes and princesses were certainly involved, but in a minor way, and in association with a lot of people in the private sector. The Shah's role was to keep an eye on them. But little by little, and imperceptibly at first, things changed. The sudden rise in the price of oil aroused appetites which would not be curbed. And since the example of those at the top inspired people at all the lower levels, in 1977 Iran provided much the same spectacle as a haunch of meat thrown to an army of starving rats.

The Weaknesses of the Shah

The Shah's apparent severity toward his family gradually melted. Today, as I try to sort out my personal memories, many of the sovereign's weaknesses emerge quite clearly. For instance, I realize that there was a strong element of jealousy in his character. In 1961 he resented the successes of Ali Amini, who although discarded kept in touch with political circles inside and outside Iran. In 1967 there was a rash of rumors in Tehran about his imminent return to power. When I informed the Shah about them in the course of an audience he shrugged and pulled a face. "Amini is no true statesman," he told me. "When I appointed him prime minister his first public statement was to announce that the country was bankrupt! A statesman doesn't say things like that. It can only give rise to unnecessary panic." He frowned and added, "Besides, when I visited the U.S. at that time, wherever I went people kept asking after the health of my Prime Minister—as if I personally was of no account!"

The Shah was always latching onto trifling details and then letting them rankle. In 1968, while we were discussing the United Nations conference on human rights which was to be held in Tehran in May, I put forward the name of Nasrollah Entezam to lead the Iranian delegation. He shrugged and said, "Why not?" Then after a pause he added, "Yes, but these people don't know their place. In 1950 he was president of the

General Assembly. When I went to the United Nations he thought that the presidency of the Assembly exempted him from his duty to kiss my hand."

He detested Nasser, who had made speeches attacking him, and he tensed whenever the name of the Egyptian President was spoken in his presence. He was critical of the American Democrats: Roosevelt because in 1943 he had compelled the Shah to visit him, whereas Stalin had taken the trouble to come and see the Shah; Kennedy because he had no great opinion of him. Iran was the only country in the world which had a "War Ministry." The reason was that during his three years in power Mossadeq had changed the name to "Defense Ministry," and the Shah could not stand his former Prime Minister.

He could not bear the prospect of anybody else acquiring popularity. There were some circles in Tehran where it was felt that he had not really been displeased by the assassination of Mansour in December 1965. Mansour had been too good an orator. Mossadeq's enormous success with the masses after the nationalization of oil put the Shah in a rage. His jealousy even extended to his own wife, whose thoroughly natural human warmth made her a popular figure. One day in 1973 the Shahbanou made a very successful speech, which was broadcast on the air, attacking flattery and in favor of freedom of speech. The Shah instructed my brother, "Tell my wife that she can't talk like that." My brother told me about the incident. "What could I do?" he asked me. "How could I interfere between them? When he doesn't dare do something himself, he saddles other people with it."

Besides this, there was a whole range of observable

contradictions in his character, so that you would hear the most varied opinions passed about him. Dean Rusk saw him, if not as a kind of genius, then at least as the best-informed man in the world after the President of the United States. Henry Kissinger saw him as an absolute but enlightened monarch; William Simon (then secretary of the treasury) as a "nut"; Cynthia Helms (the wife of the former CIA chief and ambassador to Tehran) as a complex person full of contradictions, and so on.* There is something to be said for all these judgments, but for the sake of objectivity I must add that the negative elements in his character did not surface until late in his reign, and particularly in his last eight months.

Looking back with hindsight I now feel that his greatest weakness lay in his relations with his family and friends. His brothers and sisters, nephews and nieces, brothers- and sisters-in-law often did just as they pleased, and their friends' behavior could not fail to damage the monarchy, but the Shah always forgave the members of his family and his immediate entourage. Furthermore, though he was feared by all his top civil servants and high-ranking officers, he did not dare to lay down the law to his relations. That task was always left to others. For instance, one day he was attending army maneuvers when he noticed that his brother, Gholam Reza, was wearing enormous side whiskers. He turned to his then Minister of the Court, Alam, and asked him to tell his brother either to shave off the whiskers or resign from the Army.

Another case involved his former head of protocol,

* *New York Times,* January 17, 1979.

who reportedly was doing a roaring trade in selling decorations in return for handsome "gifts." The Shah ordered him to be dismissed and prosecuted, but when the Queen Mother promptly intervened he left him at liberty and contented himself with saying that the man had better keep out of his sight from now on.

Some years previously he was visiting a new hospital, accompanied by an uncle of mine who was then attached to the court. All the beds were occupied, with doctors and nurses busy tending the sick. When they were about to leave, my uncle had to go back to get his hat, which he had left in one of the wards. He found the beds empty and the so-called patients, recruited specially for the visit, vanished. When my uncle reported this to the Shah he just shrugged and said, "Don't bother me. Let it drop." There he was quite unlike his father. Reza Shah once ordered all his governors to have trees planted in their districts. The story goes that one day he saw a palm grove planted in the desert on the Abadan road. He stopped the procession of cars and congratulated the governor, who was traveling with him. Then he took off his kepi, breathed deeply, and leaned against one of the trees—which gave way under his weight. In order to impress Reza Khan, the governor had done no more than stick the palm trees in the sand. The Shah chased him with his stick, then fired him and put him in prison. But in many other ways, father and son were much alike.

Like Father, Like Son

Reza Shah had three wives at once. His son had three in succession: Fawzia, Soraya and Farah. All I know about the first two is what I have been told, which is that both of them resented their husband's infidelities. It is said that in 1944 Fawzia surprised the young Shah in the arms of one of his mistresses, and that things went wrong between them after that. Certainly Fawzia did leave Iran in the spring of 1945, on the pretext of visiting her family in Egypt. She never came back, and some time later a court communiqué announced their divorce.

In 1946 I was assigned to our Paris embassy, where I lost touch with Tehran's high-society gossip. In 1949 Princess Shams and her husband arrived in Paris with an impressive number of dogs. The princess was accompanied by a shy young girl with big bright eyes. As usual I saw to the formalities at the airport, and I learned from her passport that her name was Soraya Esfandiary Bakhtiar. Only later did the ambassador pass on the news that she was to be the Shah's next empress. She had a German mother, and I was instructed to buy her a selection of the best German novels. Among the books I sent to Tehran were some novels by Thomas Mann, and soon after that I was summoned by my panic-stricken ambassador. "What have you done?" he wailed. "You've sent some books by a Communist writer!" My explanations had little effect—world culture didn't cut much ice with Iranian high society.

The marriage was celebrated at the Gulistan Palace, amid splendors worthy of the *Thousand and One Nights*, and when Soraya's turn came to quit Tehran in 1958 she left a spate of rumors behind her. Some said that the Shah wanted to take a second wife in order to ensure the continuity of the dynasty, which could be passed on only to a male heir. Others said that she had caught him *in flagrante*. Since the private life of the sovereign was the least of my worries, I paid no attention to the Soraya stories and the court gossip.

It was only later that I heard a few echoes of the imperial adventures. One day while I was with the Foreign Ministry, I and some other colleagues were asked by our Minister, Ardeshir Zahedi, to take a very pretty European out to dinner. These colleagues told me that Zahedi and Alam (then the Shah's minister of the court) used to arrange entertainment for their master. I never managed to verify this, but the following year in New York I happened to meet a woman friend who had spent some time in Tehran teaching English. She told me that while she was there Alam had invited her to a cocktail party at his own home. He greeted her amiably enough and showed her into the drawing room, which was empty. Alam withdrew and did not reappear. A door opened. It was the Shah. After an embarrassingly bland conversation, the young woman asked to leave.

No one I knew had anything but good to say about the Empress Farah, who was admired not only for her beauty but also for her intelligence and candor. It was she who opened the doors of the palace to art and culture, they said, and after my return to Iran in 1965 I was soon able to confirm what I had heard. I even used to wonder how she felt about living in an environment in which hardly anyone so much as opened a book and the arts were despised. Without being an intellectual she knew how important it was for a cultural and scientific elite to be given room to develop. But the Shah seldom took her seriously.

Other more crucial features of his father's character came out in Mohammad Reza Pahlavi, such as his sense of discipline and hard work, and his cardinal interest in the composition and organization of the Army. In both men one can also point to moments of compassion and to other moments of extreme cruelty. Reza Shah sometimes imprisoned former companions and had them killed. Others he sent into exile. Yet occasionally he was forgiving. There were times when his son acceded to appeals for clemency, but he was not unduly perturbed by the executions which were more common in his reign than in his father's. Of course, at the end of that reign he was to leave every one of his former colleagues in the hands of the executioners.

Like Reza Khan he became increasingly aloof, even from his own family. He spoke to very few people, except for various foreigners, and that made court ceremonial grow more and more somber.

The Wealth of the Pahlavis

Reza Shah was not averse to riches, and I have already mentioned the estates he confiscated. What about his son? How much did his fortune amount to? Some astronomical figures have been mentioned in the press. For instance, the journalist Ann Crittenden has claimed that according to sources in the banking world the Shah's personal portfolio was worth over a billion dollars, and that a substantial proportion of the two to four billion dollars transferred from Iran to the United States in the last two years had belonged to the royal family.* But according to rumor the most important source of the Shah's fortune was the Pahlavi Foundation, which was thought of as being his personal fiefdom.

Last autumn a dissident group drew up a report which alleged that the Pahlavi Foundation and the royal family had shares in most of the country's businesses. This report, which it is obviously impossible for me to check, contained a list of investments. I give it for what it is worth. It stated that the foundation or members of the family had sizable interests in seventeen banks and insurance companies, twenty-five metallurgical plants, eight mining companies, ten building-materials factories, forty-five construction companies, and so on.

The princes and princesses were paid big commissions or acquired interests through the various companies they had set up. At the end of December 1978 a list was circulated in Tehran giving details of these activities. This list revealed in particular that Princess Ashraf (or her eldest son) had picked up commissions on the contract with the international consortium GNPS, on all purchases of the Dassault Mystère 20 by the government, on the big thermal-power-station contract given to Brown Boveri, and the contract for equipping the

* *New York Times*, January 10, 1979

port of Shahar Bahar (Brown and Roote); that the Karaj highway had been diverted so as to pass through property being developed for sale to private buyers by Princess Shams; that the Society of Red Lions and Suns paid Princess Shams's traveling expenses; that Prince Mahmoud Reza, who held the concession for growing opium, resold it on the black market; that Prince Gholam Reza had holdings in apartment blocks to be built in the south of Tehran; that Prince Abdorreza was paid commissions for helping Japanese companies, and that he was involved in the cellulose-paper-factory and Tehran-underground-railway-project scandals, and so on. Of course I am unable to prove all these allegations, but the public was only too ready to believe them.

In 1977 my brother showed me documents proving that the princes had illegal business involvements. I say "illegal," because in 1959 the Shah had forbidden public servants and members of his family to take any financial interest in state transactions. My brother told the sovereign what he knew, but usually his hands were tied. Once, in 1971, the Shah did allow him to close down some real-estate agencies which belonged to the princes or to various other people in high places at court, but the effect of this move was short-lived, and it set the entire imperial entourage up in arms against my brother. After his appointment as minister of the court, Amir Abbas became alarmed about the introduction of casinos. He wanted to prohibit them, starting with the one in which Princess Ashraf had an interest. In August 1978, a few weeks before his resignation from office, he sent a photocopy of the contract for this gaming house for legal examination, looking for a way to close it down by due process of law. Gambling is against the laws of Islam, and he felt that to permit it harmed not just the Shah but the whole country. His departure meant that the question was dropped.

In any case it was an open secret all over Iran that the princes and princesses were making a mint out of their business dealings, and the knowledge did no little harm to the sovereign's reputation. I met one Indian businessman at the home of some American friends who was well informed about Iran's problems. He said that the royal family was monopolizing too many of the best business openings, and making enemies of all the people in the private sector who had been finding opportunities for making profits literally snatched out of their hands. He compared the situation with Sanjay Gandhi's business ventures.

Paternalism

Paternalism was another element in the Shah's character, and I had the opportunity to observe it in action when he visited New York in the autumn of 1969. He was giving a private lunch in honor of U Thant, then Secretary General of the United Nations, at the residence of our ambassador. I was in New York as a member of our delegation to the General Assembly, and I joined our Minister, Ardeshir Zahedi, at the Waldorf Towers.

Zahedi seemed delighted. "Everything went beautifully at the lunch. The Shah was pleased, and congratulated us. But there was a hitch over the dessert. I knew that His Majesty did not like pastries and preferred ice cream, so I unobtrusively sent a note to Homa [our ambassador's wife]. But they only brought ice cream for the King! It doesn't matter. U Thant paid no attention. But the headwaiters—and I told them so afterward—didn't serve the King and U Thant at the same time. Apart from that, everything went very well. The King was satisfied. But we'll have to find some more stylish waiters." When I asked about the conversation at table he was rather at a loss. He had been keeping an eye on the service!

(He would have made a perfect headwaiter. Zahedi's philistinism was profound. In January 1970 I accompanied him and various colleagues to an audience with the Shah to discuss the Bahrein question. Zahedi drew a few sarcastic comments from the sovereign, who told him, "You don't understand a thing. You are like Don Quixote, thinking he could fight with a wooden sword!" When the audience was over, Zahedi turned to me with a worried expression. "What did he mean by saying that I was like Don Quixote? Who is this character?")

Later we were joined by our ambassador, Vakil, who was smiling a smile of relief. "The Shah complimented me, you know. He told me that he was satisfied with my work."

Now our New York consul came up, overjoyed. "Guess what? His Majesty has congratulated me over the consulate's facilities. He is pleased with me!"

It was like being back at kindergarten. The children were jumping for joy because of a pat on the head from

Daddy. They would run a mile for one kind fatherly word. Going to the royal court was like going back to childhood, and the sovereign's paternalism radiated far beyond the limits of the court itself, and out into society in general. (Oddly enough, paternalism is just as prevalent in the new regime. What is an Imam, if not the guide and father of the people? This undoubtedly stems from our ancestral traditions. In Iranian legend, unlike the Oedipus myth of the Greeks, it is the hero Rustum who kills his son. In other words, he prevents the son from growing up and becoming the master of his own fate, an independent agent. It was against this dependence on a stifling paternalism that the youth of Iran rose in rebellion. Can our young people submit to a new paternalism?) The Shah did not see the signs. His liberalization policy came at a time when there was already a split between himself and the people, and was consequently greeted either with skepticism or simply with indifference, because the change in his character which took place in the late 1960s removed all credibility from such a move.

The Great Change

Until now I have tried to portray certain features of the Shah's character by referring to events and to some of my own memories. The resulting picture contains elements of strength, courage and weakness all at once. Overall he is not so very different from the rest. Without being ordinary, he handled his ups and downs in a more or less normal way. His situation was not always easy, but until the early 1970s he seemed not to be having much difficulty in dealing with any problems that cropped up. Like everyone else, he had his changes of mood, and naturally in his position these affected the affairs of state, but that also happens elsewhere. He allowed no familiarity and tended to keep his distance from others, and even from his friends and family. That too is understandable considering his position.

But it is clear now that the Shah's character became deeply split after the famous Persepolis celebrations. It is hard to date that split with precision. The Nixon visit in 1972 is probably a critical point, and another crucial period was that of the quadrupling of the price of oil in 1973–74, but there were clear indications long before these dates.

How is the change in the Shah's character to be defined? For my part I locate it in a certain rigidity in his decision-making, a separation from reality, and an insensitivity to human factors. Certainly this often afflicts dictators or statesmen who remain in power for a long time—a Franco or a Stalin in his later years, for example. But the Shah was still relatively young. Premature hardening of the arteries? Just power mania? I cannot say for sure.

The many interviews he gave after 1974 sometimes make one's hair stand on end. How could he admit the replacement of physical torture by methods of psychological pressure? Why those bitter diatribes against the decadence of the West? And those disparaging remarks about women and the clergy? Or his accusations against Mossadeq as an "absolute creature" of the British? All at once a crude way of speaking which is out of place in a head of state began to color his remarks. He stopped paying any attention to the susceptibilities of his audience or to the existence of public opinion. More and more he gave the impression of living in a world of his own imagining.

Schizophrenia? Delusions of grandeur? Creeping megalomania? My object in these pages is not to diagnose the Shah's illness but to underline the change of character which brought things to a head.

As early as 1969 the Shah was making some fairly extraordinary statements. Looking through my diaries, I find the following entry, dated October 2, 1969:

> Now the Shah seems rather carried away by his own dreams. He lives in the "grand designs" which he projects onto reality. Two days ago he made a speech to the officer corps to the effect that in the event of attack we would carry out a "scorched earth" policy, because if we had done that in 1941 we would not have been invaded. What was there to be scorched in Iran? The Allies did not enter the country to take possession of it; they needed a supply route. He even transforms the *realities of the past* for his grand design. He feels sure that clear heads infringe his own rights and that he can no longer tolerate what contradicts his dream. Greater weight of paternalism. Turning to pageantry and protocol . . . But then again, without the authority of the *father*, the national family will fall apart, the cement which holds so many varied elements together will give way. This is the drama of the citizens of the Third World, Iran included: they find themselves caught between the desire to grow up and the need for a father to keep the country united.

I believe that my analysis of 1969 is peculiarly applicable to the present situation. In an essay written in 1945 I argued that the entire history of Iran reflected a constant struggle between two principles, feudalism and administrative centralization. This struggle produced temporary power balances which were inevitably upset at more or less regular intervals. And I asked the following question: "Will the new balance which appears to have set in over the last forty years be equally precarious, or will it culminate instead in a solid synthesis capable of replacing the forms of the past and leading us at long last along the path of progress, thereby making up for several centuries of delay?" (The essay was entitled "The Crisis of Feudalism in Iran.") And in 1965 I really did believe that the Shah was taking us in the right direction. It seemed then that he was producing a positive answer to the question I had asked twenty years previously. That is why I and many of our friends decided, despite our different political views, to join in the national effort for economic development. Unhappily the change in the Shah's character and his fantasies of a new Achaemenid monarchy diverted him from the proper path.

Returning to the subject of the Shah's increasingly wild assertions, let us take a few random quotations from his last book, *Towards the Great Civilization*, which is crammed with examples:

> No profound change can come about in our country outside the framework of the monarchic order.

> The monarchic regime as soul, essence, existence, source of energy and foundation of the national sovereignty and unity constitutes the solid basis of the great

civilization and the strong custodian of all its values, its progress and its material and moral gains. This regime will guide and protect the destiny of the Iranian people in the most brilliant period in their history.

I have guided my people along this wonderful path of Destiny because I felt that only that path could insure their dignity and happiness. Having an absolute faith in this, it was my duty to set the nation such a goal, not only as the person responsible for its destiny but also as the father, guide and friend of every Iranian.

For thirty-seven years I have been devoting all my energies to the service of my people, and I shall persevere as long as the Divine Will acknowledges my mission. And thanks to His Favor the path I have begun will stretch onward after me; nothing but the total destruction of human civilization could stop the Iranian people on their way.

The participation of the people in all the country's affairs, and the government of the people by the people, are now a reality at every level of social life. The Iranian people freely elect their representatives to the cooperatives, village councils, local tribunals, town and district assemblies and arbitration councils. And at a higher level the people participate directly in the elections to the Rastakhiz party and in sending representatives to the two chambers of Parliament. They also enjoy full freedom of expression through the various party organs as well as through the press and information media, as a genuine democracy demands.

In order to realize the extent to which the Shah was caught up in a world of his own imagination during the last years of his reign, the whole book should be read. The jolt comes even harder because it is impossible to overlook the fact that he sometimes took his political realism well past the point of cynicism. Thus, in 1975 his sudden decision to abandon the Kurds came as a shock even to Kissinger and his colleagues. After years of strife with Iraq over the vexed question of sharing out the water from the Shatt-al-Arab River, it took the Shah a single evening to come to terms with Saddam Hussein, the strong man of the neighboring country, while attending an OPEC meeting in Algiers. Overnight he jettisoned the supporters of Kurdish rebel leader Mulla Mustafa al-Barzani, and when world opinion blamed him for turning his back he just shrugged and offered the nonchalantly indifferent explanation that the Kurds didn't want to fight anymore, they were too tired!

This story clearly illustrates the way he conducted the affairs of his country. He made his own unilateral decisions and did not even bother to give the slightest advance warning to public opinion either at home or abroad. At heart he despised his colleagues as he despised the whole world; in interviews he often referred to his colleagues as "my people." His own interests, which he readily confused with his country's, came first and foremost. In his boundless egoism, the Shah decided and the rest had only to obey.

A Great Among the Great

After the jump in the price of oil he felt entitled to do whatever he pleased. He started to behave like one of the world's "great" men. Often he would go into solitary retreat to think about the future, and he would come back with sweeping programs. That was how he thought up his "great civilization" in 1976, broadly defining it in his book as follows: "It is a civilization which puts to work the best of human knowledge and insight in order to ensure the highest material and spiritual standards for all Iranians." In sum, he was reviving his idea of a meteoric rise into the ranks of the world's most developed nations. This objective was an old obsession of his. In 1959 he had boasted to *Le Figaro*: "Give me ten years and I will make Iran a great power once again."[*]

His delusions of grandeur outstripped the realities of the country. A secret CIA report of 1976 described him as a brilliant but dangerous megalomaniac. That he was a megalomaniac became clearer and clearer. That he was dangerous he proved by his decisions.

Almost to the end he never stopped proclaiming that he would transform Iran into one of the "five industrial powers" before the start of the third millennium, and that his "great civilization" would act as a model both for the Third World and for the West, whose "degeneracy" he continued to deplore. In his haste to build up a high-technology industry he unbalanced the whole economy. His military appetites swallowed up his country's oil revenues for no productive ends.

His blind self-confidence was based on dangerously simplistic views. Two constant assumptions possessed him: that everything is possible if you have the financial means, and that Iran's income would keep on growing. He lost his temper with my brother and the

[*] *Le Figaro*, July 9, 1959.

economic experts who did not share his point of view.

There was unease about his galloping megalomania which set him into rigid attitudes. He saw the opposition as negligible: on March 22, 1976, he told *U.S. News and World Report* that his opponents were becoming violent because they could not get their way through propaganda. The Shah was offering the people his own political philosophy, he said, so the Marxists were growing desperate. He made no bones about informing Mike Wallace that the Jewish "lobby" was too strong in the United States and that it controlled the press and the media.* And he became more and more immune to Iranian public opinion. In the summer of 1976 my brother accompanied him in his helicopter on a flight that took them over Chalus, near the Caspian. My brother pointed out the villas that were being built by the head of SAVAK for sale at a high price. "There's a lot of talk about it in town," he remarked. "That doesn't matter," the Shah replied. "After all he's investing, that's good." The SAVAK boss had been given the land by the Shah himself.

My brother's modest life style displeased the sovereign, who told him one day, "You enjoy living in a pigeonhole!"

When it came to human rights he had his own version, which was very much at odds with the general international concept, since it did not apply to "saboteurs," "terrorists," "traitors" and "weeds." After 1976 there was a world outcry against the imprisonment of opponents of the regime, but, lost in his own dreams,

* *Sixty Minutes,* October 24, 1976.

the Shah no longer heard. I remember a speech on human rights delivered by the Empress before a mainly intellectual audience in the summer of 1977. Everybody applauded, but several people asked me, "Why tell us? She'd do better to speak to her husband!"

That was the Shah's state of mind some months before the events which were to bring about his downfall. There was a real iron curtain between him and reality. He had shut himself up inside an idyllic vision of the country and a court crawling with sycophants.

In 1976 he blithely claimed that he had abolished corruption. When Olivier Warin asked him whether he thought it beyond the bounds of possibility for Iran to install a republic, he answered with sublime assurance, "History will follow its normal course. It hasn't happened in three thousand years, even in the days when republics were still popular and representative and democracy meant something like stability, in a situation of peace and equality. Today I don't really see what could make a Persian think that a change of regime would do him any good." He kept telling everybody who would listen that "the opposition was himself."

In 1958, while I was making a film about Esfahan, I took my cameraman up onto the roof of the Ali-Ghapu Palace. Behind the beautifully decorated walls of the main square, the building was held up by slender rough-hewn tree trunks. Even in the days of Shah Abbas, the great Safavid king, the monarch saw only the façade!

The Harder They Fall

His divorce from reality combined with his deep belief in his own daydreams to make the Shah increasingly rigid. He firmly believed that he was under divine protection. During a childhood illness, Ali, the first Imam, the Prophet's son-in-law, appeared to him and saved him. Later on, when he was thrown by a horse, Saint Abbas appeared and held him in his arms to save him from falling onto some rocks. Later still, he even saw the hidden Imam. "No one can harm me," he liked to tell people. He felt that his role as sovereign required him to be solitary and aloof, and kept himself informed through his intelligence services. To him, opposition protests were simply a sprinkle of minor resistance, with no further meaning. He felt that things were going well and that the people were happy to follow him.

His incredible faith in his own destiny and the rigidity of his thinking impelled him to ignore every opportunity to come to terms with the moderate opposition. By the time he eventually decided to look for a compromise it would be too late.

When opposition intensified and broadened in 1978 he did not understand, and that made his awakening to reality an even ruder shock. Now that his dreams had crumbled he felt hollow and incapable of reacting. He had moments of depression, and continually vacillated between his various courses of action, leaning on the advice of his immediate entourage and the American and British ambassadors. By laying the blame on his associates and seeking foreign protection he quickly dissipated his years of accumulated pride.

Everyone now agrees that during the last eight months of his reign the Shah was not functioning. He listened to visitors but did not hear them. He had long bouts of silence and stopped issuing instructions. The country had no leader capable of evaluating the situation and reacting accordingly, and this was an even more serious defect because the royal dictatorship had inured his top officials to taking no initiatives of their own, so that even at the most critical moments they would wait for directives which were slow to arrive. Since the sovereign had got rid of all the "difficult" characters in his entourage while he was establishing his supremacy, there was nobody left to take over from him.

This state of affairs spread confusion in the government and the Army, while on the other hand the opposition was becoming more and more united and closing its ranks. In face of that growing strength the Shah grew irremediably weaker. The king who had been his country's uncontested leader suddenly became a dangling marionette, moving when his advisers pulled the strings. One of Bakhtiar's friends told me that it was the Empress who had to conduct the negotiations over forming a new Cabinet. The Shah stayed on the sidelines. In any case, by November 1978 his downfall had become a certainty.

And on January 16, in a moment of supreme weakness, he left the country, abandoning most of the collaborators who had been arrested on his own instructions in the hands of his enemies. Parviz Raji, who was the Prime Minister's principal private secretary before becoming Iran's ambassador in London, told me that my brother once pointed to a portrait of the Shah and said, "He's a selfish man. He drops you without a word, once he realizes that he no longer has a use for you!"

During the final days of the regime, when the Shah was in Morocco, some bewildered generals phoned him from Tehran to consult him about what steps they should take. He refused to speak to them.

When it was known for certain that the Shah was going, unknown to Amir Abbas one of our relatives sent him a message through an intermediary asking for Amir Abbas to be taken on the plane. The Shah made no reply, and allowed the man who had served him for fourteen years to be murdered by the new regime. On the day of that murder he kept his mouth shut, and when he opened it three weeks later it was only to attempt to clear himself by a deliberate lie. He had made no approach to my brother before he left, as I know only too well, because I was in touch with Amir Abbas right up to the moment when he decided to give himself up to the new authorities. The fact is that it was not the Shah who offered to get my brother out, but some of our relatives and friends, who set up a commando team to break him out of prison and smuggle him across the frontier. When he received their message my brother was enraged. "I don't want to run away in disgrace," he said. "I am not a coward. I am devoted to my country and I mean to defend myself publicly." A mutual friend of my brother and Shahpur Bakhtiar even told us that before leaving the country the Shah had given his approval to the course of action proposed by his last head of government. In order to save the monarchy, Bakhtiar wanted to persuade Parliament to vote to enforce Article 82 of the Penal Code (providing for the death penalty for violation of the constitution) against all those whom the Shah had had arrested by the Azhari government. In the scenario worked out with the Shah's approval, Bakhtiar was prepared to ask for the death penalty against my brother for abuses of power committed by the Shah. He was naïve enough to believe that would satisfy the people and enable the monarchy to continue. I have no reason to doubt the word of this friend of my brother and Bakhtiar, particularly when the same arrangement is confirmed in an article by Eric Rouleau, quoting statements by "an eminent Iranian jurist, and member of the Commission on Human Rights." Referring to Bakhtiar's intentions, this man told the French journalist, "The procedure he had chosen would have satisfied Western legalism, but Amir Hoveyda would have been shot all the same."*

So much for the evolution of the Shah's character in the course of his long reign. Although I have personal reasons for hating him (his responsibility for my brother's death is beyond dispute), I want to remain as objective as possible. No matter how tragic the consequences of his last actions for me and for many others, in the past there was a positive side which should not be totally forgotten.

Whatever else may be said about him, the development of the character of Mohammad Reza Pahlavi

* *Le Monde*, June 13, 1979.

showed clear signs of maturing in the early 1960s. In 1963, he braved all dangers and all obstructions to launch a program of revolutionary reforms which was to quickly improve Iran's material situation. But along the way he lost sight of his original aims; his early successes went to his head, and he failed to restore the constitutional legality which had been suspended since the *coup d'état* of 1953. He became so detached from reality that from 1976 onward he made serious mistakes in the conduct of the country's affairs, destroying the equilibrium he himself had contributed to establishing.

4

THE FINAL DOWNFALL

From the domestic viewpoint, fortunately I
have no worries.

—The Shah to *Kayhan International,* October 30, 1976

Amol, Iran, Sunday, October 29, 1978

Feeling was running higher and higher in the little town by the Caspian Sea, set in its ring of orange groves. Since the demonstrations of October 7, when the police opened fire and a number of people were killed, all sorts of rumors had been circulating and tension had kept on mounting. The townspeople's imagination was haunted by the burning of the Rex cinema in Abadan, now definitely connected with SAVAK provocateurs. On October 27, there was a whisper that SAVAK was planning to set the bazaar on fire, and students and young people took to the streets armed with clubs in order to protect the population. Those adults who did not positively encourage them made no effort to stop them. The suddenness of the reaction took the authorities by surprise and left them floundering. Some SAVAK agents were caught and handed over to the local magistrates, and the young people posted sentries at all the town entry points, patrolled the streets, directed traffic, imposed a curfew, and so on.

Although on Monday, October 30, the Army invested the town and crushed the rebellion, the incidents in Amol nevertheless marked a point of no return. The demonstrations now took on a distinctly revolutionary character. It was no longer a matter of a simple crisis, or of people being exasperated into mass protests; this was an outright revolutionary movement. In the space of ten months the Shah's enemies harnessed the generalized discontent and channeled it in a determined direction. One terrified faction in the Shah's entourage set up a hullabaloo about "the hand of Moscow." Others detected PLO influence and Kadafy agents.

All the same, at that moment it was still possible for the Shah either to abdicate or to strike some crucial blow to save his throne, at least for the time being. The Army was still under his control, as the Amol incident showed; the Americans had given him carte blanche, or so it seemed; the Russians were standing back and proclaiming the necessity of nonintervention in Iran's internal affairs; the middle classes were shaken by the violence and only too anxious for a lead to follow. But the Shah was no longer "functioning," as Treasury Secretary Blumenthal said after his visit to Iran. He gave way to fits of nervous exhaustion, and when he emerged from them he remained irresolute and hesitant. The measures he announced were utterly out of step with events, as for example when he canceled the usual receptions to celebrate his birthday, or made a donation to the victims of the Khorasan earthquake.

He also continued to miss his opportunities. He shilly-shallied so much in his consultations with the opposition that he gave Sanjabi, the leader of the National Front, time to go to Paris to see Khomeini. In the communiqué published after their meeting Sanjabi fell right into line with the Ayatollah's position.

In the meantime some of the Shah's advisers, alarmed by the events in Amol, were pressing him to take a hard line. A friend at court told me that Ardeshir Zahedi was talking about a "Chilean-style" solution, with arrests and mass executions in order to create a climate of fear. At the same time, in order to show that the Shah had decided to liberalize the regime he proposed to sacrifice as many scapegoats as possible. One man close to Zahedi told me in November that before returning to Tehran he had said in front of several people in the lounge of the Waldorf-Astoria that several "culprits" ought to be executed right away, my brother included. Another of the people there has corroborated the Washington ambassador's bloodthirsty remarks. I mention them here because they illustrate the internal strife that continued to divide the ruling class, in spite of the threatening circumstances. Instead of uniting and closing ranks as did the supporters of Khomeini, the members of the regime dissipated their strength by giving free rein to their personal ambitions. Zahedi's own ambition was to become prime minister, and for years he had nursed an insensate hatred for Amir Abbas.

The Amol incident reverberated all over the country, and there was heavy pressure on the Shah to get rid of Sharif-Emami and replace him with a tough military man. In fact, the Prime Minister was accused of having created an extremely dangerous situation by making too many concessions to opposition demands. In any case the masses were putting all the gains made at Khomeini's door.

There was more and more talk about inaugurating a

military government, but was martial law not already in force, and administered by the hawkish General Oveissi? The Shah was at his wits' end. Was he to revert to his Franco role? Yet he was still obsessed with Juan Carlos's successful efforts toward liberalization. He hesitated to come down hard on either side. Sharif-Emami knew about the "hawks" and their intrigues, and tried to resist them. Eventually his hand was forced by the military.

Tehran, Sunday, November 5, 1978

While strikes spread throughout the country, and especially in the oil fields, suddenly the troops disappeared from the center of Tehran, leaving the way clear for the demonstrators, who overturned vehicles and set fire to buildings, including the offices of the British Embassy. Everywhere cries of "Death to the Shah" went up, and there was general rioting.

The United States ambassador sent a warning to Washington about the deteriorating situation, but President Carter refused to authorize a mass evacuation of American citizens in Iran, in order not to embarrass the Shah. He continued to give public support to the regime—a few days earlier he had made a big show of receiving Crown Prince Reza, who was accompanied by Zahedi. On this occasion the President of the United States reiterated his appreciation of the Shah's efforts to democratize the country. Cyrus Vance also announced American backing for the measures taken by the sovereign to restore order.

When I read all these reports I called a well-placed American friend and asked him, "Have you really made up your minds to get rid of the Shah?" He was taken aback, and asked me what I meant. "You couldn't find a better way to overthrow him than stepping up your expressions of support. As far as Iranians are concerned, he is already an agent of yours." In fact ever since the spring the demonstrators had been calling him a "puppet in the hands of the American imperialists."

On the evening of November 5 Sharif-Emami at last agreed to resign, after two and a half months in government, with a disastrous record. A few weeks later he made a discreet exit from the country, after first liquidating and transferring abroad as many of his assets as he could.

While he pursued his consultations with Ali Amini and other politicians, after meetings with the American and British ambassadors the Shah appointed his new Prime Minister, General Azhari, his chief of staff. At the same time he made a televised statement in which he pledged himself to correct the "errors" of the past, to fight against corruption, redress injustices and restore civil liberties after the departure of the military government. He ended by saying, "Your revolutionary message has been understood. I know everything about why you have given your lives." Yet again the Shah (or his advisers) forgot that he had made promises of this type before—for instance in 1976, to eradicate corruption, and in 1977, to hold free elections. He had lost his credibility. And the Shah's belated action merely prolonged the mistakes which he had never stopped making right from the start of the troubles.

What was the good of a public confession? If he wanted to regain popular esteem by showing how frank and brave he was, he should have explained his motives in public, stressed the positive achievements of his reign, admitted his mistakes and assumed all responsibilities personally—after all, this would have corresponded to the reality of the regime. And what was the good of a military government? If it was a matter of restoring order he should have dissolved his rump parliament and showed a firm intention to organize free elections. Instead of that, the military government spent its time in getting a vote of confirmation from Parliament and looking for scapegoats.

In any case, as soon as the change of government had been announced the Army reoccupied the streets. (Sharif-Emami's supporters claimed that the troops had been taken off the streets on purpose on November 4 in order to encourage demonstrations and force the Prime Minister to resign.)

The troubles ceased in Tehran, but unrest continued in several towns. Once more the United States publicly affirmed its support for the Shah. A State Department communiqué explained that the Shah had appointed a military government under his own authority when it had become obvious that there was no chance of forming another civilian government to restore the public order necessary before elections could be held. The mention of "another civilian government" was a reference to Amini's comings and goings between the palace and the opposition, and to the fact that the latter was refusing to join in forming any coalition as long as the Shah remained in power.

To tell the truth, the Shah could have abdicated at that moment and allowed a coalition to be formed. He might possibly have rescued the monarchic principle, even though the opposition was demanding a referendum. In any case he would have saved many human lives. But owing to his selfish clinging to power, and poor advice from associates with axes of their own to grind, the Shah did not perceive the underlying reality of the situation.

Meanwhile, at Neauphle-le-Château, the Khomeini movement continued to gather strength and to direct the revolution. The old Ayatollah reaffirmed his intransigence and threatened to summon the masses to a holy war if the political demonstrations were not strong enough to overthrow the sovereign.

No one believed in the sincerity of the Shah. I talked to one influential merchant from the Tehran bazaar who was visiting New York for reasons of health, and he asked, "How can we trust the King? He wants to pull down our shops. He has increased the number of banks and big stores, and taken most of our business away." Before the modernization of the economy, in fact, the bazaars had controlled most of the country's commerce, and lent money at rates of interest higher than those required by financial institutions.

Among the lay opposition, the hope was that the Americans would pressure the Shah into abdicating in favor of his son, and that the Constitution of 1906 would be applied in full. But the Shah had Zahedi and the military looking over his shoulder, and he refused to go. The bad advice he received, together with his reluctance to take the necessary decisions at the proper time, rapidly reduced his room for maneuvering.

The Scapegoat Solution

Immediately upon receiving his appointment on the evening of November 5, Azhari had a secret meeting with Zahedi and the new chief of staff, Gharabagui. According to the account which reached my ears, during their discussion Zahedi convinced the new Prime Minister of the need to arrest a certain number of public figures in order to defuse the attacks on the Shah's person. They then drafted a list of well-known figures, my brother among them. By throwing the whole blame onto them, and then staging rapid trials, they hoped to wipe the Shah's slate clean again.

The following day Azhari obtained the Shah's consent, and on November 7 he announced the arrest of fourteen people on charges of corruption or abuse of power. Among them was the former SAVAK chief, Nasiri. On November 8, still with the Shah's consent, the government imprisoned Amir Abbas, but without mentioning any specific charges against him.

I am told that the King insisted on a quick trial in order to divert public attention, but the Justice Minister deemed that current legislation did not provide any mechanism for putting former prime ministers on trial outside Parliament itself, unless they were to be prosecuted for embezzlement or corruption. But in the case of Amir Abbas he could not think up an indictment, and it would take several months to arrange a political trial before Parliament. The King now instructed the Justice Minister to draft extraordinary legislation and submit it to Parliament as soon as possible.

Rumors circulating at that time alleged that the Shah and the Empress had asked my brother to take all the blame on himself if he wanted to save the throne. I have not been able to ascertain the validity of these rumors, but the fact that the regime was looking for scapegoats is clear.

Concerning the arrest of Amir Abbas the Shah subsequently told *Le Monde* (on April 27, 1979), "I accepted that list [of people to be arrested] except in the matter of Hoveyda, whom I summoned to the palace on November 7. . . . Broadly speaking I asked him to leave Iran at once, by a private flight, if he had to. I felt that his life was in danger. Hoveyda heard me out, then he simply replied, 'There is no question of my running away from my own country; I have nothing to blame myself for. If you see it as your duty to have me arrested, then do so, you have the means at your disposal. . . . ' I expected that answer from him: Hoveyda was never a man to duck his responsibilities, and I knew that he was free of all suspicion."

That my brother refused to leave the country when he had the opportunity is true. (Five other Prime Ministers did get out—Amini, Amuzegar, Sharif-Emami, Azhari and Bakhtiar.) But the Shah's offer to get him out is an invention of His ex-Majesty's imagination. And if he knew that my brother was "free of all suspicion" why did he permit his arrest, unless he was looking for a scapegoat? And if he feared that "his life was in danger" was it not because he knew about the role destined for Amir Abbas in the coming performance?* I have already mentioned Zahedi's cold-blooded suggestion about my brother. In any case I was in touch with Amir Abbas at that time, and I know that the Shah had told him that his arrest was just a temporary measure for the sake of saving the throne, and that he would be able to defend himself and would come out of the affair "a bigger man." I then asked Amir Abbas to reply by a statement establishing the Shah's responsibility and exposing the use of scapegoats. He refused point-blank, saying that it would only add to the country's difficulties. The following day one of our relatives telephoned from Tehran, warning me that my brother was in danger and urging me to keep my mouth shut.

In the same statement to *Le Monde*, the Shah claimed that at the time of his departure from Iran on January 16, 1979, he had given my brother the chance to "leave Iran discreetly." That is an outright lie, which is vehemently rejected by all those who were in contact with Amir Abbas during those critical days. I spoke to my brother on January 16, and I know that he received no such offer. A female relative even sent a message to the Shah and the Empress entreating them to take Amir Abbas with them in their plane. Knowing that the game was up, the Shah could certainly have taken with him those of his colleagues who had been arrested on his own instructions. That would have done something to restore his tarnished image. He chose to run. In the court of history he will be judged for what he is.

Finally, in the same statement the Shah claims that

* See Part Three.

those arrests were necessary "to quiet the mob." It is common knowledge that they had no such effect on the masses, who were after the Shah's head, not my brother's. In which case why did he not release my brother as he released Sanjabi and other members of the opposition a few days after their arrest?

No matter what the Shah says, calm did not return and the strikes and demonstrations continued. The newspapers protested against the censorship imposed by the military government by ceasing publication.

The Tactics of the Military Government

The new Cabinet decided to put pressure on the opposition. They arrested Sanjabi and one of his lieutenants and threatened to jail the "ringleaders" of the workers' strikes, particularly in the oil fields. The government's intention was to scare the opposition into negotiating with the Shah. It aimed to muster as much support as possible behind the original demands of the Shah's opponents, namely the full and strict application of the Constitution of 1906.

This tactic was doubly unproductive. For one thing, the opposition had grown stronger since September, and had no great fear of minor skirmishes. (As the Shah soon realized when he ordered the release of Sanjabi the following week.) For another, the military government lost credibility by showing its hand. The whole opposition now knew that the government was military only in appearance, and that under the table it was looking for a compromise. They hardened their attitude, and rated the Shah much weaker. They also thought that the Americans had no intention of saving the monarchy at the price of a civil war.

So the newborn Azhari government was blown. Moreover, on November 10 there were violent clashes between police and demonstrators in Ahvaz and Abadan. The 35,000 oil workers demanded higher wages and the release of all political prisoners, whereupon the government ordered them back to work and threatened to fire them if they disobeyed. Sanjabi's National Front called for a general strike on Sunday, November 12. Many of the oil workers who had been forced back to their posts adopted slowdown tactics.

On November 16 the Army fired on demonstrators in Behbehan in the south, Mashhad in the northeast, Esfahan in the center, and Sari near the Caspian. Some demonstrators were killed and many injured.

While the opposition continued to gain in strength and to extend its influence over the masses, the court only made more miscalculations. Thus, on November 17, Army Day, the troops paraded in Tehran, but for the first time in his history they did so in the absence of the Shah. Fear and consternation were the natural public conclusion about the sovereign's state of mind. Most observers felt that he should have put on a bold face and shown himself in public on that occasion, thereby proving his own determination and at least giving a boost to military morale.

On November 18 the Empress went on pilgrimage to Najaf and Karbala, Shi'ite shrines in Iraq. The official version was that she was going in response to an invitation from the Iraqi government, but in fact the motive behind the visit was crystal clear—it was a gesture to demonstrate the royal family's attachment to the state religion. But it came too late, and was received either with indifference or with downright hostility by the masses. If the Empress had made the pilgrimage in July, as originally planned, she might have gained some sympathy, but the visit had been postponed precisely because Khomeini was in residence in Najaf at the time.

Still, on November 18, General Azhari presented his government before Parliament. For a public which saw the Chamber of Deputies as a puppet show, this was just a joke. And it is hard to see who was supposed to fall for it. Already the new government had lost its "military" character.

And to cap it all, on that same day Moscow broke its silence on the subject of Iran for the first time. Brezhnev declared that the whole thing was a strictly domestic question, and warned against any outside interference, thereby drawing a sharp reaction from President Carter.

On the nineteenth, in a placatory gesture, the Shah freed 210 political prisoners, while the Army faced demonstrations in various parts of the country.

It will be obvious that the basis of the Shah's policy had hardly shifted at all since the start of the crisis. He simply went on wielding the stick and carrot. And if the Tehran bazaar did open its doors again, it was only to make up for the losses suffered during the strike. "The government is mistaken if it thinks we're giving up the fight," said most of the merchants.

And in fact there were violent demonstrations in the

big towns. On November 19 the soldiers opened fire on the crowd in Shiraz. On the twenty-third, after clashes in Mashhad, troops invaded the hospital and brutally finished off the wounded. On the twenty-sixth the workers responded to the call from religious leaders and the National Front to protest against the events in Mashhad; countrywide strikes and demonstrations included the oil workers.

The Situation at the End of November 1978

After three months of continual unrest and labor stoppages the economy was on the verge of paralysis. The banks were functioning only sporadically, and there was a general shortage of liquid cash. Imports, many of them perishable, were piling up in the ports and at frontier crossings as the result of the strike of customs officials. There were slowdowns in the factories. The civil servants were twiddling their thumbs behind their desks, when they were not staying home. And the flight of capital continued.

At this moment a long list of public figures was circulated, containing the names of people (including members of the royal family) accused of having smuggled their assets out of the country during the previous months. It was said to have been issued by striking employees of the Central Bank, although it was left unsigned. Among the 144 names it contained were those of Amuzegar, Zahedi and many other officials. The figures quoted looked markedly exaggerated. Some of the people indicted went to the Prime Minister to ask for an inquiry into the facts of the case, but for reasons of its own the government did not follow up their request. As far as the public was concerned, no proof was needed.

So the opposition's tactics seemed to be working. They were trying to implicate and discredit as many as possible of the Shah's supporters, using any means that came to hand. Azhari's arrests of prominent figures were met with jeers, not applause. "The Shah doesn't know which way to turn," they said, "so he's trying to lay the blame on other people." The opposition was only too happy to see the Shah undermining his position by creating strife in his own ranks.

Nevertheless there was apprehension among both the supporters and the enemies of the regime as they waited for Moharram, the month of religious mourning, which began that year in December. They expected a decisive confrontation on the eleventh, the day of Ashura, which commemorates the martyrdom of Imam Hussein, the Prophet's grandson. The "loyalists" reckoned that if the Shah managed to turn this corner safely he would survive. The opposition was certain that the day would shatter the monarchy beyond recovery.

From his lair in Neauphle-le-Château the Ayatollah Khomeini redoubled his exhortations, interviews and maledictions. In palace circles in Iran, as well as in various world capitals, there was astonishment at the attitude of the French government, which was allowing the exiled cleric to incite a rebellion, contrary to the international rules governing political refugees. In fact, when Khomeini arrived from Najaf the French government had consulted the Shah, and received a request not to turn him out.

In Washington, while Brzezinski went on encouraging the Shah, other members of the Administration assessed his chances of survival as "bordering on zero." Doubts were emerging in the sovereign's mind about the true intentions of the Americans.

In Iran, realizing the powerlessness of the Azhari government, some of the military had started to consider staging a coup when the proper moment came.

But an objective evaluation of the situation late that November makes it clear that there was no possibility of saving the monarchy, either by resorting to repression or by seeking to establish a constitutional regime. The Shah and his advisers had fumbled all the opportunities presented to them in September and even as late as October.

The Azhari government was already doomed.

The Month of Moharram

On the night of December 1–2, the eve of the month of religious mourning, the faithful spent the evening in the mosques in the customary way, then flooded into the streets, defying the curfew imposed under martial law, to cries of *"Allah-o-Akbar"* (God is great). In the south of the town they were cheered on by the populace, massed on the rooftops. The Army did not react.

Next day, thousands of people came out after the curfew, wrapped in white shrouds. The soldiers opened fire, killing more than sixty people and wounding many more. By way of protest, hundreds of thousands of workers and civil servants went on strike.

The Shah had been living in almost total solitude for a week. Apart from a handful of intimates, and consultations with opposition moderates or the United States ambassador, he saw no one. According to information which came to me from a member of his entourage, he was afraid of a confrontation. He was longing for a civilian team to take over from the military, who had turned out to be incapable of "quieting the mob." They could not make decisions, and came running to him with their most trifling problems. The Shah would not accept that it was he himself who had spent years training them to refrain from independent action. It was he himself who had kept them on the fringe of the nation's life, so as to prevent them from being contaminated by liberal ideas. And now he was asking them to manage the country's affairs. Prime Minister Azhari confided to a friend of mine, a top official in the Economic Ministry, "The ministers keep asking me to make decisions, but I know nothing about these problems of economics. I'm a soldier!" One foreign diplomat just back from Tehran told me, "The Shah is finished. He'll never be able to retrieve a shred of credibility. By arresting your brother he has lost the confidence of his own supporters. Already there's grumbling in the Army. Most of the officers feel that if he has dropped his best servant and friend, he'll do the same to them."

Ardeshir Zahedi sped off to Tehran to "boost the Shah's morale." One of my colleagues jeered, "With an

adviser like that, he's bound to fall." Tongues had been
loosening for some time by then. Nobody was afraid of
SAVAK surveillance anymore, and nobody doubted
that the regime was on its last legs. My colleagues were
openly critical of the monarchy. They refused to have
anything to do with Princess Ashraf, the head of our
delegation to the UN General Assembly, who in any
case was cautious enough to stay shut up in her private
town house.

For the first time, foreign observers had begun to talk
not about a crisis but about a revolution. The Americans were putting out feelers to Khomeini through
"private" emissaries, and the former U.S. Attorney
General, Ramsey Clark, and Professors Falk and Zonin
visited Neauphle-le-Château. Various Iranian politicians also contacted the Ayatollah, in an effort to stave
off the collapse of the regime. Washington was still
making a show of official support for the Shah, but was
embarking on a reevaluation of its policy on Iran. The
imperial system was audibly tearing apart at the seams.
The world's governments were debating all the obvious
questions. Would the crippled Shah hold out? Would
the Army stay loyal to him?

Every now and then I heard from my brother. We
could not talk openly, of course, but we didn't have to
spell things out to each other. There was no accusation
against him as yet; the promised trial was long over-
due. Why did he not issue a written defense? He did
not want to embarrass the Shah. I told him all I knew
about the Shah—his depression, his hesitations—but
my brother still refused to believe me. For the first time
I began to fear for his life.

Meanwhile, after two nights of bloody demonstrations a relative lull intervened, troubled only by isolated incidents. Azhari tried to conceal the scale of the slaughter, estimated by the opposition at over seven hundred dead. He blamed foreign subversion and the Tudeh (Communist) party, which had been banned for a long time. Yet everybody acknowledged that without the mullahs who were relaying Khomeini's watchwords, no one would have been setting foot on the public highway. And now the Ayatollah was calling on the soldiers to desert.

On December 3, pressed by the Army and encouraged by the Empress, his collar loose around his neck, the Shah made his first public appearance for several weeks to visit the air cadet training center. He tried to smile in order to hide the signs of strain that ravaged his gaunt features.

The oil workers resumed and intensified their strike, and the level of output fell rapidly, while a spate of incidents and demonstrations occurred. In his first press conference General Azhari put on a serious voice to declare, "Every true Iranian is for His Majesty." He conceded that during the thirty-seven years of his reign a few "bad things" had happened, but Iran had made great strides in road- and harbor-building, education and prosperity. It would take "more than two hours," he added, to chronicle "the great achievements" of the Shah. (As I scanned the report of that press conference I felt as if I were dreaming. How could a man be so removed from realities?)

Washington still backed the Shah, but the Administration asked George Ball, Undersecretary of State under Kennedy and Johnson, to undertake a study of the Iranian situation and to make recommendations.

(In his report, Ball was to condemn the Shah's regime and insist on the necessity of an immediate return to civilian government.) At the same time the Americans began a discreet evacuation of the families of Americans working in Iran.

On December 7 there was a hint of a change of tune in a press conference given by President Carter. In response to a question from a journalist, he said that the United States would prefer the Shah to go on playing an important role, but the decision belonged to the Iranian people. Public opinion at once concluded that the Shah was being ditched. The court intervened, and the President retracted his statement and insisted, on December 12, that his policy of support for the Shah remained unchanged.

In the meantime Sanjabi was released by the government as a token of good faith, but still rejected any possibility of cooperation with the "illegal" regime of the Shah.

It appeared that things were not working out, and, alarmed by the prospect of a major confrontation on the day of Ashura, the Shah beat a hasty retreat and gave permission for the demonstrations planned for Sunday and Monday, the eleventh and twelfth of December. By avoiding the trial of strength he was signing away his kingdom. The populace was made aware of its own power, while the Army found itself demoralized.

"He is afraid, and the Americans haven't got the nerve," people thought. The Army announced that it would stay clear of the demonstration route, and would intervene only in the event of disturbances. The religious and lay organizers of the demonstrations asked the participants to remain calm.

Tassua and Ashura

Shi'ites all over the world signalize the ninth day of Moharram, the eve of the assassination of the Imam Hussein, and the tenth day by processions of mourning.

On Sunday, December 11, the day of Tassua, hundreds of thousands of people (some sources put the figure as high as a million) held a procession in the center of Tehran, marched into Shahreza Avenue and headed for Shahyad Square, where the sovereign had erected a monumental arch in 1971, celebrating the 2500th anniversary of the monarchy. But in an unprecedented development the banners fluttering above the heads of the crowd indicated not only mourning for the martyr of Karbala, but also a political purpose. Huge portraits of Khomeini, Mossadeq and Shariati were carried high. Slogans against the Shah rippled in the wind —"Death to the Shah!," "Death to the American cur!," "Traitor Shah!," "With Allah's help we will kill the impious traitor," "Victory is near," "Khomeini is our leader," and so on. People from all walks of life could be found in the throng—workers, intellectuals, merchants from the bazaar, women with or without the concealing chador, clerics in black, green or white turbans, children, adolescents, the wealthy in European dress, the poor in rags. The discipline and calm of that human tide astonished all observers.

Next day the people of Iran flooded onto the main

streets of their principal towns in millions. Except in
Esfahan, where violent clashes occurred, they all
showed the same calm, the same discipline, and above
all the same determination.

Ayatollah Shariat-Madari, the most eminent religious authority inside the country, explained to one
journalist, "In the absence of provocation, the people
protest nonviolently. The very scale of the demonstrations shows that the whole nation is behind our demands."

But the Shah and his advisers seem not to have realized the deep significance of these events. By evading
the trial of strength they believed they had won a
breathing space. The solution they envisaged remained
the same: a coalition government with the opposition
participating, within the framework of the Constitution of 1906. But Sanjabi, the only valid candidate outside the clerical establishment, refused to take part as
long as the Shah remained, and the latter not only refused to abdicate but was determined to retain absolute
control of the Army. Backed by the high-ranking officers and by Zahedi, he dug in his heels. What went on
in the palace beggars the imagination. While the
masses were demanding the departure of the Shah,
while Khomeini's intransigence hardened, and while
the opposition was consolidating its strength, the Shah
and his advisers, closeted behind the heavily guarded
portals of the Niavaran Palace, discussed the command
of the Army and studied plans which had long since
been overtaken by the movement of events. It was By-
zantium all over again.

At that point it is just possible that the abdication of
the Shah, the appointment of a regency council con-

taining both lay and religious members of the opposition, and the dismissal of all those people, inside or outside the Army, who bore the slightest responsibility for the bloody repression of the demonstrations, might still have saved at least the principle of constitutional monarchy, if not the regime. But the Shah and his advisers were blindfolded by the imaginary world they lived in; they were going round in circles. Their basic assumption, that the monarch must stay on the throne, had already been discarded by the opposition. Before the Ashura demonstrations the massive use of force might have turned the Shah into another Pinochet. The Army was still cohesive and powerful, but things had changed once it was decided that the troops should stay away from the demonstrators. The officers started wondering about the loyalty of their men, while the people were reminded of their own strength. The Iranians ascribed the Shah's seclusion to fear, and they emerged victorious from those two days of religious mourning.

From then on came a sequence of alternating threats and withdrawals. And with every passing day the delusions of the Shah's advisers further eroded the chances for a constitutional monarchy, even without the Shah and his dynasty.

My Brother's Situation

As I say, my brother occasionally called me on the phone, but we could not exchange any important information. He had no contact with the Shah, who never even inquired after him, according to friends at court. For essential matters I used the good offices of a woman relative who was allowed to visit my brother once a week. We were both agreed that the sovereign no longer had any chance of survival, and that it was he who was responsible for his own royal plight. My brother was also aware of Zahedi's maneuvers, and said that he had enough information in his possession to neutralize him, but was unwilling to produce it yet, so as not to increase the sovereign's troubles. "I know so many things," Amir Abbas said, "but I can't say them now. All right, so the Shah has behaved badly toward me, but I'm not the type to turn my coat at the last minute. I shall say it all in my memoirs."

Alas, they did not give him the time. His jailers' haste to destroy him puzzles me to this day. Why refuse him a public trial? Why refuse him the month he was asking to write his memoirs? According to one eyewitness who was present at the mock trial he endured, he recognized two of his so-called judges behind their masks. According to the same witness, one of them was Yazdi, one of Bazargan's ministers, and the other was Garabagui, one of the Shah's generals. How is this to be verified? The witness adds that they did not even trouble to take him before a firing squad, but killed him in his cell.

The same source states that the "court" had let it be understood that it would give my brother the time to write his memoirs, but that fifteen minutes later, after consultation with "higher authorities," it decided to liquidate him. Why? What were they afraid of? Would my brother's disclosures have damaged the new regime? Would they have affected people close to Khomeini? Or was it the fallen sovereign who was being protected? Were there agents of the old regime in the ranks of the new?

Other disturbing questions also come to mind. For instance, how was it that Yazdi's son-in-law, who was in charge of our Washington embassy and claimed to have found documents compromising Zahedi and various American VIPs, refused to make them public? Sanjabi is supposed to have resigned from the Bazargan government over this affair. Yazdi's son-in-law was refusing to send him the papers in question. Where are they now? Who was being shielded? The Americans involved? Or was it Zahedi?

But as well as my brother's there were other names on the Tehran death list who might have made sensational disclosures. Generals Nasiri and Pakravan were former bosses of SAVAK; knowing the relationship between the Shah's security police and the Israeli secret services and the CIA, they could have yielded all sorts of crucial names and information. Similarly Khalatbari, the former foreign minister, knew the inside story of the Shah's foreign policy. But instead of getting them to talk, it is as if the idea was to make sure that they did not. So what was being hidden? Whose interest lay in covering up the true facts about that period in the country's history?

There are other outstanding questions. How is it that people appointed or backed by Zahedi are still at their posts, both at home and abroad? And why do the new authorities never breathe a word about Amuzegar, under whose government many demonstrators were killed by the Army? I do not claim to know the answers to these questions, but there is cause for suspicion in the fact that Zahedi supported Nixon against Kennedy in the presidential elections of 1960. (Which is why he had to be transferred to London after Kennedy was elected.) There was a rumor that Zahedi, then our foreign minister, made contributions to the Nixon campaign in 1968, with dollars brought in by special diplomatic courier. Speculation aside, however, there can be no doubt that my brother's papers could have thrown light on a good many of the darker areas of recent Iranian history.

I make this digression at this point in the narrative in order to establish that a great deal of mystery attaches to the rapid collapse of the regime. No minor part of that mystery is the role played by our ambassador in Washington. I have it on good authority from American friends that the planners in Washington had no great respect for Zahedi's political acumen, while a French journalist who saw the Shah in Rabat told me that the Shah too had no faith in the competence of his former son-in-law. Yet the press was full of the ambassador's commuting between Washington and Tehran. Did he make a knowing or unknowing contribution to the overthrow of the monarchy?

Historians will have a hard time getting to the bottom of these riddles. I am asking questions which I am unable to answer. What is certain is that by mid-December the game was up for Mohammad Reza Pahlavi, Light of the Aryans, second in the dynasty of the Pahlavis. With the Ashura demonstrations the days of the monarchy were clearly numbered.

Death Throes

News of the Esfahan demonstrations reached the public a day late. The opposition march started peacefully, as it did in Tehran and other cities, but then a group of demonstrators broke away and attacked and burned the local SAVAK headquarters. Thrown back by the police, they spilled out into Chahar-Bagh, the main avenue of the former capital, and broke windows in the banks, cinemas and police stations. They also pulled down statues of the Shah and his father. The troops who had been withdrawn from the center now returned in force and opened fire on the rioters, who nevertheless went back into action next day when "loyalists" tried to put the statues back on their pedestals.

At the same time the majority of oil workers refused to go back to work after the Ashura ceremonies.

Meanwhile Ayatollah Khomeini gave an interview during which he threatened to cut off oil exports to countries which supported the Shah. He went on making political statements, despite a warning from the French authorities, and called on the Iranian people to observe a day of mourning the following Monday, in memory of those killed in Esfahan.

On December 13, the Army put on a demonstration in Esfahan on behalf of the Shah. Trucks, buses and cars crammed with soldiers and peasants rolled through the streets to shouts of "Long live the Shah!" and forced motorists to display portraits of the royal family on their windshields. Similar demonstrations went on in other towns.

In the days that followed, the religious and lay opposition were active again in most of the big towns, while the Shah still persevered in his efforts to form a coalition government.

Even more than the mass demonstrations, it was the strikes which hit the regime by undermining the economy. Prime Minister Ashari stated that the unrest was costing the nation more than sixty million dollars a day, and that the government was running short of money.

On December 15 the United States made it known for the first time that, without wishing to intervene in Iran's internal affairs, its representatives were trying to help the Shah to establish a civilian government. This action was based on the recommendations made by George Ball. Amini suggested setting up a regency council, but Zahedi and Oveissi, the martial-law administrator, advised the Shah to reject any such solution.

Under these conditions, and in response to American pressure, the sovereign called in a former minister of Mossadeq's, Gholam Hussein Sadiqi, to undertake a mission of exploration.

Signs of unrest were appearing in the ranks of the Army. On December 18 troops refused to fire on demonstrators in Tabriz. A few days previously soldiers had entered the officers' mess in a Tehran barracks and opened fire at random.* Conscripts deserted in Mashhad and Qom. The higher-ranking officers were at sixes and sevens about the course to be followed. These de-

* According to usually reliable sources, the officers killed belonged to a faction in the Imperial Guard determined to prevent the Shah's departure.

velopments disconcerted the Americans and the Shah's personal circle.

The day of mourning ordered by Khomeini was observed throughout the country on Monday, December 18. It passed off quietly in Tehran, but there were clashes in Tabriz and Qom.

On December 20 the Shah and his wife went skiing near Tehran. It was the sovereign's third venture out in all of three months. His entourage wanted to give the impression that he was still cool and confident.

Sadiqi was unable to convince the members of the opposition to join in forming a coalition government, and on December 22 he threatened to give up trying. Tehran swarmed with rumor after rumor of an impending military coup.

When the Shah and the Empress arrived back at the palace, the sun and fresh air of the Elburz Mountains had restored a little color to the sovereign's cheeks, but his morale was at its lowest ebb. He skulked inside the walls of the Niavaran Palace rather like Hitler in his bunker. Now and then there would be a scrap of news to revive his hopes momentarily—President Carter renewing his expressions of support, or demonstrations in the Shah's favor in Kurdistan or Esfahan. The rest of the time he gave in to bouts of gloom. No one knew whether he was thinking or sleeping.

In fact in his lucid moments he sensed that the end was coming. His wife and advisers kept him informed about the secret negotiations they were holding with some members of the opposition, including Bakhtiar, in the hope of helping him to pull out of his depression, but the effect was only to intensify his despair. After all, just a few months earlier he had been calling

Sanjabi and Bakhtiar traitors worse than Communists, and now he was having to cling to all the people he most detested. For a man who in August had been an undisputed dictator, that was the worst humiliation of all.

Meanwhile anti-American feelings were running high among the population. In Ahvaz, in the south, an American citizen, a director of operations for a consortium, was killed in an ambush, while in Tehran students demonstrated outside the American Embassy to shouts of "Death to Jimmy Carter!" The marines guarding the embassy dispersed the demonstrators with tear gas.

Sanjabi followed Khomeini's lead by stating before a National Front meeting that calm could not return without the departure of the Shah. Oil production fell to 700,000 barrels, and the flight of capital accelerated on the black market, where the dollar sold at well above the official exchange rate. There was a shortage of heating oil, and the government brought in rationing.

On December 27, Tehran suffered a day of violence occasioned by the funeral of a young teacher killed by soldiers on the roof of the Ministry of Higher Education. Although the procession had received official authorization, it came up against the Army, and demonstrations ensued. The exodus of Americans working in Iran was speeded up, and unrest continued over the following days.

It appears that during all this time the Shah's advisers were hoping that the renewed violence, the gasoline shortage and the disastrous state of the economy would exhaust the people and bring them round to seeing the monarchy as the only hope of restoring order. It was the opinion of every observer that this was an utterly childish expectation.

That being so, on December 29 Sadiqi abandoned his efforts. The Shah now appealed to Shahpur Bakhtiar, the vice-president of the National Front, to attempt to form a government. After several weeks of consultation with the palace, he was now ready to accept on the express condition that the Shah should set up a regency council and leave the country. Ardeshir Zahedi, who had risen to become the Shah's recognized adviser and spokesman, denied the reports of the Shah's intention to leave the country. He also repudiated rumors about the departure of the Queen Mother. Next day she arrived in Los Angeles with an extensive retinue.

It was announced in Washington that the President had ordered the aircraft carrier *Constellation* to leave its base in the Philippines and to be ready to make for the Persian Gulf if required. (It returned to its home base very soon.)

On the thirty-first, Ambassador Sullivan denied that there was to be any massive evacuation of American nationals; in the same breath he advised them to return "temporarily" to the United States.

That night, General Azhari tendered his government's resignation. The Shah asked him to take care of current business until a civilian Cabinet could be formed.

At the turn of the year the situation was looking hopeless. The general strike was paralyzing the whole economy. The closure of the central bank had halted all transactions. The shops were shut, and staying shut. Tens of thousands of people were having to queue for hours on end outside the distribution centers for heating oil, in order to collect their ration. The demonstrations continued, and shooting could be heard here and there.

The palace was a hotbed of illusions. One spokesman told journalists that the people had had enough of these disorders and were protesting against those who inflicted such privations on them for political reasons. The Shah's advisers were still hoping for a popular backlash against the opposition!

In fact the workers and civil servants were grimly determined to prolong the strike until the Shah got out. Curiously enough, food supplies continued as usual.

Khomeini in Neauphle-le-Château and Sanjabi in Tehran spoke against the formation of any government with allegiance to the Shah.

Violence continued in Tehran and the other big towns. Oil exports came to a complete stop, and the airports closed down.

It was under these conditions that the curtain rose on the final act of the tragedy.

The Departure of the Shah

Confusion reigned in the higher ranks of the Army. They knew that their personal futures were still bound up with the Shah's, and were worried by the prospect of his exile. The hardliners joined with Zahedi in his efforts to dissuade the sovereign. The rest played for safety by transferring their assets and their families abroad.

On January 1, 1979, Bakhtiar, who was putting his Cabinet together, publicly reaffirmed the Shah's commitment to leave the country as soon as the new team had been formed. Zahedi at once summoned the press to the Niavaran Palace to meet the sovereign. So the contradictions inside the regime persisted, and prevented the Prime Minister designate from deriving the maximum advantage from the Shah's promise. Instead of its producing a shock effect, public skepticism was just further enhanced. Trying hard to smile, the haggard Shah allowed the photographers to take pictures. He said how tired he felt, and expressed the wish to take a vacation, if "the situation permits."

While strikes and demonstrations went on paralyzing the country, while Air Force personnel took the place of the civilian flight controllers at the Tehran airport, while sporadic outbreaks of violence erupted all over the country, and while the tempo of the foreign exodus accelerated, the Senate and the lower chamber voted their approval of the appointment of Bakhtiar. Washington asseverated its "continued support for the Shah," and Moscow orchestrated its media campaign to prepare Russian public opinion for the collapse of the regime. An important member of the Central Committee of the Communist Party wrote in *Novy Mir*, under the pseudonym of Boris Vesnin, that what was happening in Iran was "a specific explosion of the national patriotic conscience. We are dealing here with a growth in the spontaneous historic activities of large masses who only recently had no active involvement in politics."

Acting on their own initiative, some Army officers embarked on punitive expeditions against the population in Mashhad, Qazvin, Gorgan, Kermanshah and other places. The climate of violence which seemed to be setting in throughout the country augured nothing good for the new Prime Minister.

Rumors of an Army coup were more and more widespread. It appears that General Khosrowdad, a fervent loyalist, and several other high-ranking officers were planning to overthrow Bakhtiar and seize power after the Shah's departure. They even envisaged the possibility of full-scale civil war, and were counting on the regular army, and the Imperial Guard in particular. These rumors disturbed the Americans, and at the beginning of January they dispatched General Huyser, the deputy commander of the NATO forces, to Tehran with the mission of dissuading the military from trying to mount a *coup d'état*. Immediately on arriving he entered into urgent discussions with the Army leadership, while Washington was advising the Shah to take a long vacation abroad.

On January 5th President Carter, West German Chancellor Schmidt and British Prime Minister Callaghan flew to Guadeloupe for a summit meeting, at the invitation of French President Giscard d'Estaing. According to my own information, the German Chancellor and the British Premier argued that the Shah had to be supported at all costs, whereas Carter and Giscard felt that it was no longer possible to do so in the current circumstances. However, they managed to reach agreement on how best to safeguard their respective interests in Iran. France, which had given asylum to Khomeini, hoped to be able to act as go-between with the Iranian opposition.

According to sources close to the French presidency, it turned out at this meeting that the Americans had been taking a Khomeini victory for granted ever since November, and had encouraged, if not instigated, "private" contacts with the Ayatollah and his entourage. Their numerous expressions of support for the Shah had been mainly designed to bamboozle the Saudis, by making out that the United States was not going to abandon its friends.

Meanwhile in Iran there was a rash of insistent rumors about General Huyser's mission. Some opposition circles thought that he was assessing the odds and resources for a coup. Others reckoned that he was in charge of dismantling America's secret installations to prevent them from falling into Soviet hands. Still others spread rumors that Huyser was trying to get the Iranian Air Force to send all its F-14s to Saudi Arabia.

Officially the United States affirmed its intention to cooperate with the new civilian government that Bakhtiar was supposed to be presenting at any moment. Actually there is every indication that the Americans did not give much for the new team's prospects. All the same, Bakhtiar plodded on with his final consultations about forming his Cabinet, while the Shah and the Empress went skiing in the vicinity of Tehran.

On Saturday, January 6, the Shah came back to see Bakhtiar, who presented the fourteen members of his Cabinet of technocrats. Not one member of the religious or lay opposition was prepared to participate. Instantly Khomeini, in a letter read out in the mosques, denounced Bakhtiar and asked civil servants to prevent the new ministers from entering their offices. He ordered a day of mourning on Monday in memory of the victims of the recent demonstrations.

As had to be expected, the rioting continued amid

the rumors of an Army coup. Bakhtiar pursued his consultations with the Shah with a view to forming a regency council. Washington repeated its advice for the Shah to leave the country for the time being, and recommended the military to drop any notion of a *coup d'état* and throw its support behind Bakhtiar.

On January 13 came the creation of a regency council made up of men loyal to the sovereign. Khomeini retaliated by naming a group which was to tackle the groundwork preliminary to instituting an Islamic government. With the restoration of press freedom, newspapers resumed publication.

On January 16 the Shah's departure triggered an absolute carnival of rejoicing in the streets of Tehran. In the few minutes which elapsed after the radio broadcast the news, just about the whole population of the capital thronged into the streets, to cries of *"Shah raft!"* (The Shah has gone). People embraced one another. Cars honked their horns. The scale of the response and the spontaneity of an entire nation's rejoicing impressed every outside observer. The crowd fraternized with the soldiers, while demonstrators pulled down the statues of the sovereign and his father. Slogans rang out on all sides: "Our party is Allah's party, and our leader is Khomeini"; "The final victory is the Islamic Republic"; "After the Shah, it's Bakhtiar's turn."

At the airport the haggard Shah told Bakhtiar, "Your government has my complete confidence and I hope that its members' patriotism will enable each of them to bring their difficult tasks to a successful conclusion."

The task in question was the restoration of order and the salvation of the monarchy. Bakhtiar had the Army to take care of order. To save the monarchy he was ready to sacrifice to the people those whom the Shah had singled out and jailed under the Azhari government. If they condemned to death a former Prime Minister, a former head of SAVAK and a batch of ministers and officials, the Shah would be cleansed of his sins, and then he could return.* That is why the sovereign told those officers in the Imperial Guard who threw themselves on their knees and begged him to remain, "Don't worry, I won't be away for long." Yet again he was deceiving himself. The Shah's supporters and the moneyed classes did not fall for these fine words. They knew that a chapter was ending, and they packed their bags and quietly followed the Shah's example.

The monarch was received as a head of state by Egyptian President Sadat. He said that he was going to take a short holiday in Egypt.

The staffs of all Iranian embassies abroad held meetings and voted to join the opposition. They took down the royal portraits and informed the Foreign Ministry of their intention. In New York my colleagues issued a communiqué stating that they no longer recognized Princess Ashraf as president of the Iranian delegation to the United Nations General Assembly.

In Tehran and in every other town in Iran the population celebrated the departure of the hated King and called for Khomeini's immediate return. Cries of "Long live the Islamic Republic of Iran!" went up on all sides.

On the seventeenth the rejoicing continued. The opposition did not recognize the Bakhtiar government, and demonstrators demanded his resignation. As the Ayatollah had ordered, in most branches of the admin-

---

* See p. 172, "The Scapegoat Solution."

istration the civil servants locked out the new ministers.

Bakhtiar tried to stay calm and bring things back to normal. He was counting on Army support—after all, the Shah had advised his generals to support him—but the officers felt that the Shah had written them off, and for that reason they bore a grudge against him in their hearts.

The End of the Monarchy

At Neauphle-le-Château the imperturbable Khomeini congratulated the Iranian people and asked for demonstrations against the "traitor" Bakhtiar on Friday, January 19. He rejected President Carter's appeal for him to cooperate with the new government.

On the nineteenth millions of Iranians marched in Tehran and the other main towns, to shouts of "Death to the Shah." In the capital a mass resolution adopted by acclamation at the end of the day swore to go on fighting until the Islamic Republic had been established. It proclaimed that the Bakhtiar government was illegal and demanded the resignation of all members of parliament and of the regency council.

Rumors spread in the capital about negotiations being held between the Army and the supporters of Khomeini. Hardliners in the officer corps were still discussing the possibility of a *coup d'état*. The Ayatollah announced his imminent return to Iran and demanded the revision of all contracts concluded by the Shah with foreign countries.

In Washington, Zahedi declared to the press that for the sovereign to come to the United States in the present circumstances might be interpreted as an act of abdication. That was why he would be visiting another country (Morocco) after Egypt before his eventual return to Iran. In concert with the Washington ambassador, the Imperial Guard and crack troop units organized maneuvers in their Tehran barracks in order to exhibit their state of readiness for all contingencies.

In the Iranian capital on January 23, Bakhtiar offered to resign if the Ayatollah delayed his return and left it to the people to decide on the nature of the future regime, whether republic or monarchy. But the National Security Council took it upon itself to close down the airport so as to prevent the return of the exile. On the twenty-fifth the government organized a meeting in favor of the constitution: fifty thousand people gathered in Baharestan Square in support of Bakhtiar.

But next day there was another demonstration by the supporters of Khomeini, and troops fired into the crowd, killing about fifteen people.

On the twenty-eighth, Bakhtiar offered to go to Paris to meet Khomeini and discuss the country's future with him. The Ayatollah insisted that he must first resign.

Over the following days the demonstrations continued and produced some violent collisions. The toll of dead and wounded grew. Finally, having run out of options, Bakhtiar decided to reopen the airport as a gesture of conciliation and allow the Ayatollah to return.

On February 1 an Air France charter plane flew the

religious leader back to Iran after fourteen years in
exile. He arrived to a delirious welcome as millions of
people massed along the route taken by the Mercedes
van which carried him. The crowd exploded with joy.
The procession headed for the Behechté Zahra cemetery, where the graves themselves were buried beneath
a flood of humanity. Khomeini mounted the rostrum to
a roar of acclamation and spoke in his neutral mono-
tone: "The parliament and government are illegal. . . .
I shall shut their mouths and appoint a government
relying on the support of the people. . . . Bakhtiar will
be arrested if he does not resign. . . . " He attacked the
United States and called on Army officers to join hands
with the people.

Meanwhile the Shah left Egypt for Morocco, where
students protested against his presence.

The End of Bakhtiar

Because he could not do otherwise, Bakhtiar gave official permission for the demonstrations in favor of the
Ayatollah. He also announced several measures which
were borrowings from the program developed by
Khomeini in France—revision of foreign contracts,
stopping oil sales to Israel and South Africa, and so on.

Ever since coming to power Bakhtiar had been at the
mercy of events, and he increasingly fell victim to the
same incertitude as the Shah. He was without popular
backing, and the Army obeyed him only with reluc-

tance. The measures he did take came in fits and starts and were mostly ignored. Thus, for example, he announced publicly that Zahedi had been recalled from his post in Washington, but did not inform the State Department and virtually left the former ambassador to continue in office. He announced that the people arrested were to stand trial, but did nothing to set the wheels in motion. He gave the impression of a weak man incapable of laying down a clear course of action.

On February 5 the Ayatollah took his first step as de-facto head of state. He published a decree appointing Mehdi Bazargan as prime minister of the provisional government of the Islamic Republic, and instructed him to form a Cabinet and to lose no time in organizing a referendum on the creation of the new republic. On this occasion he delivered a speech in which he called on "the whole nation to demonstrate peacefully throughout the country to express its support for this rightful Islamic government." Those who acted against him were threatened with "the punishment of Allah." As "violators of Islamic law" they would be subjected to all the rigors of religious legal process. He also emphasized that by their unanimous demonstrations and the many martyrs they had sacrificed the people had given him their endorsement as head of state.

The firman entrusting the government to Bazargan opened with the words "In accordance with the instructions of the Council of the Revolution . . ." It was the first mention of that council, whose composition is still a secret to this day.

Bakhtiar retorted next day that he did not recognize

the "so-called" government instituted by the Ayatollah and that he intended remaining at his post until the forthcoming elections, even if all the members of Parliament resigned as Khomeini was asking. He went before Parliament and presented two bills, one of them dissolving SAVAK and the other instituting a jury charged with investigating officials accused of corruption or abuse of power. In the field of foreign policy he announced his government's intention to withdraw from CENTO.

Fortified by Khomeini's appeal, Bazargan confronted the Army and Bakhtiar with expressions of mass support: more than a hundred thousand people held a peaceful, orderly march in his favor in Tehran and the rest of the country to shouts of "Long live Khomeini," "Long live Bazargan," and "Death to Bakhtiar." The armed forces underlined their presence by overflying the processions with aircraft and helicopters. But on the same day Yazdi announced that several Army units had gone over to the new Islamic government. And he upped the tempo by declaring that large-scale marches would be held in Tehran and other towns on February 8, just when Bakhtiar was due to give a press conference.

Meanwhile in Tehran the rumors of an impending military coup were becoming insistent. The United States ambassador encouraged his subordinates to make contact with the religious leadership. On February 8 over a million people demonstrated in Tehran to demand the resignation of Bakhtiar. He swore that he was not going to allow himself to be pushed around and denounced Khomeini's plans as "medieval."

But on February 9 the violence resumed. Elements of

the Imperial Guard surrounded airport technicians demonstrating in favor of Khomeini. More than fifty men were killed.

A friend who left Tehran a few days after the Shah's departure told me that he had been tipped off that the Imperial Guard was planning a *coup d'état*, under the leadership of a group of high-ranking officers.

On February 10 matters deteriorated. The Imperial Guard attacked an Air Force barracks which had come out in support of Khomeini. The occupants came out and armed the demonstrators, who put up makeshift barricades. A pitched battle continued until early next morning, with a death toll of over two hundred. According to my own information this was the much vaunted coup attempt initiated by General Khosrowdad and a few other staff officers. According to some reports it seems that one of these officers, General Rabii, gave Khomeini's supporters advance warning (though this did not save him from the firing squad). The same sources report that the whole thing was arranged with the sovereign's approval. (A few days previously the opposition had revealed the existence of a tape recording of a meeting between the Shah and his commanding officers, during which the monarch urged them to rise in rebellion. The Shah's entourage denied these allegations.)

Also on February 10 I received a call from my brother. He expressed his disillusion with the Shah's conduct. How could a true leader abandon his post like that? All those years he had been mistaken about the sovereign. It was the last time I heard my brother's voice.

In the early hours of Sunday, February 11, the Army leadership resolved to drop Bakhtiar. Receiving no more instructions from their supreme commander (the Shah), divided about the *coup d'état* suggested by Khosrowdad and a few others, and bearing in mind the advice of the American General Huyser, they proclaimed their *neutrality* in the "rivalry" between the two governments and instructed their troops to return to barracks. Bakhtiar was helpless without the support of the Army, and acknowledged that fact by taking to his heels. (Later on it emerged that he had left the country and found asylum in Europe.)

For almost forty-eight hours the capital fell into the hands of various factions obedient to no precise authority. The warders of the prison which held my brother and some of the other people arrested by the Shah vanished as if by magic, and some of the prisoners escaped. My brother stayed—"Somebody had to show a little courage, after all." He had already refused to allow himself to be broken out of jail by an action group organized by some friends and relations. He made a telephone call to Khomeini's headquarters and decided to give himself up to the new authorities in the hope that there would be a public trial in which he would finally have the chance to explain himself.

Armed units loyal to Khomeini found and arrested General Khosrowdad.

It was the end of the Pahlavis, and the end of two and a half thousand years of monarchy.

The provisional government of the Islamic Republic moved into the offices left vacant by Bakhtiar. The United States announced its intention of getting in touch with the new authorities in order to safeguard American interests. The Soviet Union officially recognized the new regime.

Tehran, Monday, February 12, 1979

As he took his opponent's last pawn off the board, Khomeini spoke the traditional phrase: *"Shah mat."** Then he leaned back and allowed his tired eyelids to close for a moment. He had won the marathon game started in 1960, interrupted in 1963 and resumed in 1978. From now on the country was his. No one could contest his authority any longer.

* This Persian expression, which goes back to the Sassanid era and is the origin of the phrase "checkmate," literally means "The Shah is dead."

EPILOGUE

The mockery of a trial to which the new authorities subjected my brother had been going on in secret since the previous day. The whole performance was a throwback to the Middle Ages and the Grand Inquisition—"judges" hiding their faces behind masks, members of the revolutionary Komiteh ranting against the accused, an indictment preferring charges of "war against God," "sowing corruption on earth," and so on. How is a man to answer accusations which have more to do with metaphysics than with law? In the preceding pages I have already written about that hasty trial, concocted with no lawyers, no witnesses, and the death sentence decided well in advance. I am still stunned by my brother's murder (how else to describe that parody of justice?) minutes after the high-speed deliberations of his so-called judges. On March 15 he told the men who dared not show their faces, "We have all lived within the same system. I therefore find myself just as guilty as all of you, for we all accepted that system. . . . '' And on April 25 Prime Minister Bazargan echoed these words on the occasion of the murder of General Gharani, his chief of staff, when he said, "Officers and soldiers cannot be accused of treason purely because they served under the Shah. We are all guilty of having cooperated, willingly or not, with the old regime."

Paradise Island, April 7, 1979

The Shah and his family swam in the warm waters of the luxury seaside resort, and tanned themselves in the sun. A few days earlier they had let themselves be photographed with smiles on their lips by the international press. When the ex-sovereign learned of my brother's murder he said nothing. He went on minding his health and devoting himself to his favorite sports of tennis, water skiing, jogging, golf and so on. For weeks he remained silent. Then, with the European press attacking him for not having lifted a finger to save Amir Abaas, he issued a statement on April 27 in an attempt to clear himself of the accusation.

But nobody was deceived by the Shah's gesture, because the fact is that he bore full responsibility for all his actions. As he was fond of remarking to every willing ear, it was he and he alone who made all the big decisions.

In 1975, referring to his intention to raise Iran to the ranks of the great powers, he told John Oakes, "It won't be the first time that we in this country have made the impossible possible."* Three years later the impossible came true—not the Shah's dream, but Khomeini's. Unarmed against an overequipped modern army, the revolutionaries put an end to twenty-five centuries of kingship and installed an Islamic republic. It was a revolution without precedent, uniting as it did the most disparate social groupings behind the two slogans of "Allah is great" and "Death to the Shah!"

From what source did the inarticulate and often illiterate masses derive their inexorable strength? Was it simply from the fervor inspired by their deep faith? But Shi'ism had been their driving force ever since the sixteenth century. Was it from the fiery speeches of Khomeini? But the Ayatollah had been calling on them to rise up in rebellion long years since.

Who helped them to rebel? Mossadeq's National Front? The intellectuals of the right and the left? But these represented only a very small minority. Or was it the oil companies, unhappy with the Shah's policies? But their powers were limited, and after all they were still getting their oil.

There has been some talk of foreign influences. The Shah held all-day consultations with the American and British ambassadors. The Palestinians trained guerrilla groups. Radio Peyké Iran had been criticizing the Shah from an East European country. Nixon and Kissinger had encouraged the Shah to squander the country's wealth on sophisticated armaments.

Other observers go further still. Thus, Robert Dreyfuss and his colleagues on the *Executive Intelligence Review* see the Iranian revolution as stage one in a grand "conspiracy" engineered in certain British and Western

* *New York Times*, September 30, 1975.

intelligence circles and designed to destabilize the region and dismember its component countries, so as to reconstitute them inside new frontiers. According to them, the Iranian executants of this secret plan were Yazdi, Ghotzbadeh, Bani-Sadr and Amir-Entezam. Again according to them, Yazdi, an American citizen, was recruited by Richard Cottam, professor of political science at Pittsburgh University, with reputed CIA connections. So it is not Western governments who are behind the alleged conspiracy, but a secret "brotherhood" whose purpose is to prevent the industrialization of the Third World and to keep it in a permanent state of underdevelopment. Islamic fundamentalism is supposed to have provided the plotters with a powerful weapon for inducing such a backward step. Iran was chosen first because conditions were favorable there. Soon it will be the turn of other countries.*

These views have found a certain amount of confirmation inside Iran itself. For instance, when the Ayatollah Taleghani, the religious leader of Tehran, disappeared on May 17, 1979, after the arrest of his children by the Komiteh, some fantastic rumors broke out in the capital. When the Palestinians occupied the offices of the Israeli representatives in Iran, according to rumor they found documents which established the existence of contacts between Yazdi, Ghotzbadeh and other associates of Khomeini and foreign intelligence services. They at once called Taleghani's son and handed the papers over to him. The Komiteh, which was tapping the line, picked up Taleghani Junior as he

---

* See *Executive Intelligence Review*, New York, February 20 and May 8, 1979.

left the building and took away the compromising documents.

These are just rumors, of course, but certain recent world happenings do give grounds for reflection. For example there is the sudden switch by Western economists, who are now talking about the bankruptcy of their previously held theories of development. All at once they are urging the Third World to confine itself to a predominantly agricultural economy, in order to increase food production and use more of the work force. And this comes at the very moment when the experts are maintaining that at the present rate of population growth the poor countries will never be able to supply their own needs. The famous "green revolution," launched amid such a fanfare of publicity, has been unable to solve the problems of the developing regions. As for Iran, with its lack of arable land and water it cannot hope to become agriculturally self-sufficient. Although the Shah may have made a lot of mistakes, the fact remains that his broad idea of industrialization was essentially correct. For how are sixty million Iranians to be fed and clothed as they enter the third millennium, once the oil deposits are used up, except by means of an export-oriented industrial sector?

No matter what one believes about the theories of foreign intervention in Iran's affairs, there is no denying that the Shah did all he possibly could to bring about the collapse of his dynasty. His armaments policy, the corruption in his entourage, his ruthless repression and stifling dictatorship gnawed like a cancer at his whole system, especially during his last two years in power. Blinded by his own dreams of grandeur and walled off from the realities of the country, the Shah ignored popular aspirations, despised the clergy, and antagonized both the world and his own people simultaneously. As I have attempted to demonstrate in the course of this book, with the help of his family he was the true and certain author of his own downfall.

Revolution was inevitable: during its last two years the monarchy flouted both law and tradition with unbelievable nonchalance. The regime could claim many tangible achievements between 1965 and 1977, but in the eyes of the poorer classes they were invalidated by the way the Shah allowed his friends and relations to line their pockets with impunity by monopolizing the nation's business. Even among the more prosperous classes there was open criticism of the sovereign's person and his political choices. The dictatorship was a dead weight on all sections of society, and public opinion saw the Shah as embodying everything that went wrong. That is what explains the immense hatred he aroused among the masses after 1978.

But is it not likely that the issues will be distorted once again by the introduction of "God" into a conflict among men who are trying to settle problems of economic justice and political liberalization? Early this century, instead of the parliamentary regime desired by both laymen and clergy, who rose in rebellion against the absolutism of the Qajars, revolution led to the dictatorship of Reza Shah. Will the return to strict Islamic law be any more liberating?

The question remains open. Listening to the news coming out of Iran, one might be tempted to believe in the perpetuation of the disorders and upheavals of

1978, with their aftermath of anarchy and discontent. And even the patriarch of Qom acknowledges that this Islamic government which he is seeking to establish reigned for only a few years, thirteen centuries ago, in the lifetime of Mohammad.* Will Khomeini do any better than the companions of the Prophet, who were unable to maintain that government? Will he understand that human societies are not to be ruled by decree?

For the present the debate developing inside the new republic remains as *totalitarian* as the one staged by the monarchy, despite the replacement of "great civilization" by "Islamic government." Sooner or later, will it produce the same reactions?

And as I ponder all these questions I find myself wondering whether it would not have been better to allow the Shah to leave the country for good in 1953. The *coup d'état* inspired by the CIA only delayed Iran's natural course of development. If Mossadeq had carried on after 1953, would Iran not have become a stable democratic state? At the time there was much ado about the "Communist threat." Did it really exist? The USSR had only just tested its first H-bomb, whereas the United States already had an impressive number. And the events of the postwar years have shown the caution of the Russians—Stalin evacuating Azerbaijan in 1945 in face of Truman's determination, and Khrushchev shipping back the Cuban missiles after Kennedy's warning. And we know from Tudeh party defectors that in 1953 their leadership prevented an armed uprising under pressure from Moscow.

* His vision of the "Islamic Republic" remains just as vague as the Shah's with his "great civilization."

All the same, the coup of 1953 only postponed the reckoning. Twenty-five years after his triumphal return to Tehran the Shah set out once again along the road to exile, but this time with shame and dishonor, leaving his closest associates in the hands of his enemies as he fled. He was captain of the ship, and he abandoned his post to save his own skin.

Truly Mohammad Reza Pahlavi's was a strange destiny: the man who succeeded in crushing revolution abroad (in Oman) was blown away like a straw in the wind by the insurrection of his own people. It is true that no man is a prophet in his own land, but with just a crumb of courage he could at least have ended his reign with dignity.

POSTSCRIPT

Now that this manuscript is completed, I feel exhausted. It is not easy to remain calm when recalling a tragedy which affects one personally. Often I have found my hand trembling at the end of the day. My whole being has been suffused with anger. With every page I grew more and more keenly aware of the Shah's search for a scapegoat in the person of my brother. And yet I have had to try to curb my feelings so as to attempt to remain objective. No other book of mine has cost me so great an effort.

To tell the truth, I had given no thought to writing about the events in Iran. After the tragic death of Amir Abbas I had intended to return to literature and painting, in order to forget that painful episode in my life. But the Shah's misleading statement to *Le Monde* on April 27, 1979, nauseated me. I therefore accepted Lord Weidenfeld's suggestion to write this book, knowing that the task would not be an easy one, but knowing, too, that I had to cry the truth aloud, if only to correct the record. I owed at least that to the memory of my brother, a brave man who refused to run away, the innocent victim of the excesses of a dictator who chose to take refuge behind others in his attempt to vindicate his own crimes. And I owed it to the Iranian people, who have the right to know the truth.

Bridgehampton, September 1979

The fears which I expressed in my epilogue are beginning to be realized. Not only has all hope of liberalization vanished, but the provisional government is leading Iran into a regime of which the fascist character is daily more marked. Its vindictiveness, intolerance and repression far surpass the excesses of the preceding dictatorships, and in its hatred of the Pahlavis the new regime has destroyed even the positive advances of the last fifteen years. With each passing day economic paralysis, anarchy and corruption take a greater hold on the fabric of the nation. The country is threatened by weakness and disintegration. The new privileged class, the clergy, has turned the revolution entirely to its own advantage, seeking to impose dictatorship by snuffing out any opposition. If the Iranian people do not wake up soon, their long struggle against oppression will be brought to an end by the establishment of a monstrous tyranny without precedent in modern history.

In this book I have tried to recall some of the roots of

the revolution. I hope that my modest contribution will help to open my compatriots' eyes to the reality of today. And I also hope that strengthened by experience they will know how to block the path of fascism and at last impose a true democracy, founded on justice and equity, respecting our traditions and our particular needs.